Great Art and Architecture in European Churches

SPLENDORS OF

DMITRI KESSEL

Commentary by Henri Peyre

CHRISTENDOM

EDITA LAUSANNE

PRODUCTION EDITA LAUSANNE

Printing
Imprimerie Centrale Lausanne and
Héliogravure Centrale Lausanne

Color engraving
Clichés Actual, Bienne; Schwitter, Bâle

Binding
Maurice Busenhart, Lausanne

First Published, February, 1964
Second Impression, September, 1964

To Manya

TABLE OF CONTENTS

PREFACE

Dmitri Kessel is well known in many lands as one of the most talented—and most ubiquitous—of the world's leading photographers. Born in 1902 in the Ukraine, he soon was to learn, along with other men of the same generation elsewhere, that violence can offer unique insights into the nature of mankind for an individual who can observe, reflect, and communicate with others through his art. He was only sixteen when he watched a mob of Ukrainian peasants kill an entire squadron of Polish cavalry which had been pillaging their village. Characteristically, he took pictures of the slaughter. For a time he served as a cavalry officer with Ukrainian forces. He emigrated to the United States and there began his career as a professional photographer. At the beginning he was especially fascinated by men working with huge machines and he devoted much time to photographing them. "Like circus trainers teaching a monster to behave" was the way he described them.

He began to work for "Life" magazine in 1937. The magazine sent him all over the world. During World War II he worked in the Atlantic on a U.S. destroyer escorting troops to Africa and Europe. He covered the Aleutian campaign in the North Pacific. In 1944 he was in the Middle East with the British Army and he photographed the liberation of Greece. Later he spent some time in postwar China.

In 1949, he photographed the modern Catholic church at Assy, in France. That same year he worked in Istanbul, sharing the excitement of the late Dr. Thomas Whittemore, the American archaeologist who found art treasures in Sancta Sophia which had for centuries been covered over with plaster. He has since photographed most of the outstanding religious sanctuaries of the ancient and contemporary world. A fervent lover and collector of art himself, Kessel has excelled in capturing, and enabling others to see and enjoy, that artistic beauty which has been defined as "a logic which is perceived as a pleasure."

He is also a skilled and patient technician. The photographs of the churches reproduced in this volume required months of arduous labor. In some cases elaborate scaffolding had to be put up, technicians had to be secured and power lines brought in after involved and endless negotiations with local authorities. To get some of his pictures Kessel had to be not only the photographer as artist but the photographer as engineer and international diplomat, too, able to harangue and persuade bureaucracy in many languages.

Dmitri Kessel has long made a specialty of photographing notable churches. In addition to those represented in this collection of his marvelous photographs, he has done perhaps two or three dozen more. And a case could probably be made for the inclusion of most of them in a portfolio of "Splendors of Christendom." The selection of the churches represented here was made on the basis of a number of considerations. It is a personal selection, but not an arbitrary one. Space was one of the overriding factors. It was not intended in this book to include all the greatest, or the most famous churches. And no effort was made to limit it to the greatest and most famous. No effort was made to cover all the styles or all of the countries where Christianity has inspired splendid buildings. Considerations of space made it necessary to leave out a number of countries entirely. All of the New World is omitted, as are Spain and Portugal, Russia, Northern Europe and the Low Countries. Some churches are here because it was felt that they could not be omitted on any grounds. Some are here because they represent their period and their style at their peaks. Some were chosen because they are great—and at the same time relatively unknown.

For the Byzantine period Sancta Sophia in Constantinople is generally considered the greatest building. In addition, it offers the excitement of hidden treasures fairly recently discovered. The churches of Ravenna—Sant'Apollinare in Classe, Sant'Apollinare Nuovo and San Vitale—are rich in early Byzantine mosaics. St. Mark's of Venice, the latest example of Byzantine art in this portfolio, illustrates the transition from the Byzantine rounded domes and emphasis on mosaics to the arches of the Gothic. Four examples of the Romanesque period are included. The Church of St. Magdalen at Vézelay is at once the oldest and the most famous edifice of the period. As for the Cathedral of St. Lazarus at Autun, it is generally conceded to have the finest examples of Romanesque stone sculpture. The Church of San Zeno at Verona, on the other hand, is noted for its metal sculpture, while the abbey of St. Savin is admired for its splendid Romanesque frescoes.

For the Gothic style it was decided to have French, German and English examples, and the choices were made accordingly. The Cathedral of St. Etienne at Bourges is believed by many experts to be a purer example of Gothic than Notre Dame, which blends some elements of Romanesque with Gothic. It was selected in preference to Chartres because it is less well known—and deserves to be better known. The Minster of Ulm was chosen for its wood carvings, one of the outstanding features of Gothic architecture. The Cathedral of Wells was chosen both for its beauty and for its striking inverted arches.

The baroque seemed best exemplified in the work of Giovanni Lorenzo Bernini, that producer of astonishments at St. Peter's in Rome. Here, in a sense, the photographer concentrated "more on the man than on the church" which is the product of so many talents. And the Church of Our Lady at Zwiefalten was picked because it shows the rococo style at its most extreme.

The least original period of Christian art is that comprising the late eighteenth and the nineteenth centuries. Music, painting, poetry, and fiction then sprang to the fore and expressed the moods and aspirations of that age. Some of it was inspired by religious faith. Much of it was secular, often positivistic in character and reflected the anxieties of men worried by what they viewed as God's absence. In the middle of the twentieth century, however, a surprising revival of religious architecture and of the arts which should be associated with it (sculpture, painting, tapestry, mosaics) has taken place. France, where that movement has yielded the largest number of works of the first order, is represented here through the Church of Our Lady of All Grace at Assy, and England by a cathedral which is unparalleled, both as Christian art and as a symbol of faith in a world reborn from the scars and ashes and, literally, the ruins of World War II: St. Michael's of Coventry.

Accompanying Dmitri Kessel's photographs—sometimes luminous, sometimes powerfully dramatic, but always striking and fresh, even when the subjects are familiar—is a commentary intended to enhance the reader's appreciation of the pictures. The commentary is the work of Henri Peyre, who has been associated with many universities including Lyons in France, Cairo in Egypt and Chicago, Bryn Mawr and Yale in the United States.

His text of course positions the churches and their works of art with reference to their periods and their styles. But the emphasis is on people: those who built or designed or sculpted; those who commissioned the artists and the architects; those for whom the buildings and the art were created to serve as an integral part of their daily religious life. And so the commentary tells of great emperors and of empresses who wielded even greater power than their husbands; of barbarian invaders who came to destroy but stayed to accept the faith; of noblewomen who had many holy edifices built in gratitude for miraculous preservation from death; of sculptors with an astonishing range of talents and equally astonishing productivity; of husbands fearful that their wives might be tempted to adultery. Here are nameless shopkeepers of the Middle Ages and a German bell founder with a lovelorn daughter; cowardly Honorius and fierce Alaric; Gislebert and Giovanni Lorenzo Bernini; Theodora and Gallia Placidia; French burghers rich enough to buy exemptions from the restraints of Lent, and lepers, feared enough to be excluded from the common worship.

These men and women were Christian. The mysteries of the creation of the world, the stories of the ancient patriarchs and of the Prophets as the anticipators of the Savior, of the three Magi, the birth of Christ, the Crucifixion and the Redemption, the visions of the Book of Revelation, the story of the Virgin—these were the subjects which moved their hearts most intensely and which their artists represented. Those were mysteries and in a sense, as modern students of religion have expressed it, man is a creature "who believes in things he cannot comprehend." But the saying of St. Anselm, the Italian-born Archbishop of Canterbury in the eleventh century, is even truer. "Credo ut intelligam" was his formula: Man believes so that he may understand. An American critic and poet of our time, Allen Tate, has expressed it just as appositely: "Man is a creature that in the long run has got to believe in order to know, and to know in order to do."

Some of the elements which were once part of religion no longer satisfy some of us today. History records superstition, narrowness, fanatics choosing not peace but a sword, intolerance and persecution of those who belonged to another religion. Theology, for which men once fought and died, has lost its grip on us: ideology and politics, for better or for worse, have replaced it. But the images which artists painted or sculpted as a tribute to their faith, the churches which they erected to express the perfections of God have survived and command our perennial admiration. There was often a didactic message in that art, concretely made plain for all to understand, even the simplest minds, or hidden behind symbols.

Our age knows that if man is unavoidably a religious creature, he is also fundamentally an esthetic creature. The creation and the enjoyment of beauty are well-nigh universal in mankind: from the Lascaux caves to the Easter Island carvings, from the pyramids to the Seagram Building, men of all continents have felt impelled to seek and to create beauty. There is at least as much yearning for the beautiful today in mankind as there is irresponsible ugliness in the soiling of our cities, of our river banks, of our countrysides. Photography and, as André Malraux has put it, the "imaginary museum" which reproduces and juxtaposes the art of many eras in one illustrated volume, have immeasurably enriched our awareness of the past. Today, with art much more readily accessible to millions of men and women, we may take comfort in the reassurance that our species gains in the understanding of its long past and that modern man is even more a preserver and a creator than he is said to be a destroyer.

THE EDITORS

REGAL EXALTATION

BYZANTINE CHURCHES

For over five hundred years—until the style which we call Romanesque and consider the successor to Roman architecture emerged in Christendom—Byzantine art, with its twofold inheritance from ancient Greece and from the Orient, provided Christianity with its most original buildings and its most sumptuous decorations. Constantinople, the meeting place of Asians and Europeans, situated where several sea and many land routes converged, was the cradle of Byzantine art. From there Byzantine culture spread to other regions of the Mediterranean and to the whole Balkan peninsula. Some of its most significant creations were achieved in northern Italy, in Sicily (Palermo and Cefalù), in Greece (Athens, Daphne, Mistra, Salonika, Mount Athos), in what are now Yugoslavia and Russia, in Syria and Asia Minor. It acknowledged no geographical limits; also, it refused to bow to the passing of time and its chronological boundaries are almost impossible to determine. It appeared in the fifth century, with some of its most perfect works, as though it had no need of the time for the slow growth by which childhood usually reaches maturity. The touching and naïve awkwardness which appeals to us in the archaic arts of most other nations—Egyptian, Hellenic or Western European—does not appear in Byzantine art. Its most grandiose achievement, St. Sophia, was built at the beginning of its ten-century-long history, in the years 532-537. Thanks to the flowering of Byzantine culture which took place then, especially under Justinian (527-565), Constantinople was preserved from the Huns, other barbarian invaders too were kept at bay, and the dream of Justinian almost came true. He dreamt of nothing less than the reconstitution under his aegis of the Roman world which had declined and fallen in its Italian homeland.

But Justinian wasted too much energy and too large a share of the Byzantine empire's resources in the attempt to attain that goal. His successors, especially those who came after the eighth century, lost several of their provinces to the Lombards in the west, to the Arabs in the east and south, to the Slavs in the Balkan peninsula. Thanks to a solid administrative structure, Byzantine institutions and culture withstood many blows, the most ruthless of which were dealt by the Crusaders with assistance from the spiritual sons of Byzantium, the Venetians, in 1204. The schism of 1054 severed the Eastern church from Rome and broke the unity of Christendom. But to Byzantium must go the credit for preserving a profound religious spirituality for the Eastern peoples and of winning Slavic nations to the Christian faith.

Since the turn of this century, historians have debated whether early Christian art had its origin in Rome or, as an Austrian scholar named Strzygowski contended, in Egypt, Syria, Asia Minor, and especially Iran.

In truth, while inheriting much from the East, the art of Byzantium imparted a Hellenic cast to its inheritance. For many centuries, the adjective "Byzantine" could be counted on to touch off endless squabbles over questions of the theology, legislation and politics of that ancient culture. Much of this discussion was merely the sterile pedantry of scholars and academicians who had lost contact with real life. The historian Gibbon dismissed the whole world of Byzantium as tedious and saw it as monotonous. So the turbulent but instructive and fascinating history of the sovereigns of Byzantium long remained a closed book to Westerners. Yet the conspiracies, assassinations, riots, military revolts, the occasional display of debauchery, cruelty and reckless ambition in that history have many a parallel in the annals of Rome after Caesar, of the Italian republics, of England in the late Middle Ages, of the France of the religious wars, of the Russia of Peter and Ivan the Terrible.

The artistic splendor bequeathed to posterity by Byzantine civilization was long ignored by scholars of the West, who looked upon it as a mere decline from the glory and the beauty that was Greece. The profusion of its decoration and the glittering luxury of its mosaics were not understood in their religious context: they were colorful, even gaudy, because their purpose was to depict the glory of another world and to offer an anticipatory glimpse of the sojourn of the blessed. But Byzantium suggested to most of our forebears merely formality and stiffness; Byzantine art was seen only as a series of scintillating processions on mosaics which reveled in gold and precious stones. A few poetic minds with sharper insights divined the aspiration to the sublime, that yearning for stability in the midst of a universe addicted to change that lay at the source of Byzantine art and culture. W. B. Yeats was among these perceptive ones; in two of the most celebrated poems of our age, he hailed Byzantium as the symbolic and heavenly city toward which he sailed in dream. He invoked the wise men surrounding the majestic emperors, as depicted on the mosaics of St. Sophia and Ravenna:

"O sages standing in God's holy fire
As in the gold mosaic of a wall...
Consume my heart away; sick with desire
And fastened to a dying animal
It knows not what it is."

In "A Vision," the poet clarified in prose his conception of the city of his dreams: "I think that only in Byzantium, maybe never before or since in recorded history, religious, esthetic and practical life were one; that architects and artificers... spoke to the multitude and the few alike. The painter, the mosaic workers, the worker in gold and silver, the illuminator of sacred books were almost impersonal, almost perhaps without the consciousness of individual design, absorbed in their subject matter, and that the vision of a whole people."

Such a vision of Byzantium may have been as unrealistic as Keats' vision of Greece; but it helped send many moderns back to the treasures of Byzantine architecture and painting. Certainly Byzantine civilization was far from being afflicted with premature senescence. It lasted for eleven hundred years. Except in the valleys of the Nile, the Euphrates and the Ganges, in areas where time appeared to have stopped while the West feverishly accelerated the pace of history, a thousand-year ascendancy such as was enjoyed by Byzantine culture from 330 to 1453 is unknown. It was not born weary and aged. It did not produce an art wholly severed from life, or scornful of men's efforts to wrestle with fate, or unmindful of the good which can be achieved and enjoyed by humanity before eternity engulfs us. Byzantine art, like many of mankind's accomplishments in the realm of the beautiful, stemmed from a protest against death and the impermanence of mortal creatures.

The enduring influence of Byzantine churches is visible around us today in several continents. Domes and cupolas have become familiar features of ecclesiastical architecture. Modern craftsmen have revived the workmanship of mosaics, which the artists of St. Sophia, of Ravenna, Sicily and Venice had practiced with unequaled mastery. The non-figurative art of our time, the retreat from reality among the moderns, their flight away from the rendering of the human face in its changing nuances, these often recall the achievements of Byzantine creators. The challenge of bigness, that curse or blessing of modern architects, was a challenge to the builders of St. Sophia, one of the largest churches in Christendom; they met it successfully, to produce perhaps the greatest of all the monuments of Christian art. We may experience a purer mystical emotion at Chartres or in some small Franciscan church in Tuscany. We may feel closer to the primitive spirit of Christianity under the vaults of a Romanesque shrine. The sculptured porches of Gothic cathedrals or the colorful marble façades of Italian churches hold a more vivid appeal to many men of the West. Still, the grandiose interior of St. Sophia strikes most observers with awe. A century ago, long after the Turks had replaced the cross with the crescent in Constantinople's churches, the French traveler and writer, Théophile Gautier, praising St. Sophia above all other Christian sanctuaries, went so far as to declare: "Byzantine architecture is most certainly the necessary form of Christianity."

Early Christians forbade making images of the divine; they had inherited the Judaic tradition prohibiting effigies. St. Paul, in his famous visit to Athens, upbraided the Athenians for their fondness for sculptured representations of their many divinities. Tertullian, one of the most impassioned Latin Fathers of the Church, declaimed against rendering through art the mystery of Christ's passion: "The more splendid that mystery, the deeper it should lie in darkness, so that the difficulty of understanding Christ's death and resurrection would lead to appeal for God's grace." God being spirit, in the view of those early theologians, He could not be portrayed through any material object.

But symbols soon crept into the Roman catacombs, then into the squares and churches of Byzantium: the symbol of the Cross, the rites of the Last Supper and of the Eucharist, and the Good Shepherd. Daniel in the Lions' Den became one of the motifs which Constantine ordered depicted in his capital. The Sacrifice of the Lamb recalled the Lamb of the Book of Revelation. The Passion of Christ and the Last Judgment became alternately tenderly moving or austerely majestic motifs in Byzantine art. The Redeemer Himself, Who had not been portrayed in the early centuries of Christianity, was at first given some features of a pagan god, of an Apollo, and represented without a beard. It was not until later that He became the bearded Christ, with eyebrows almost touching each other, the stooping figure familiar in Christian art.

For many years, Byzantine emperors ruled over an efficient administration and levied taxes over a vast dominion. Funds for building and decorating were therefore plentiful. The emperors surrounded themselves with a rigidly ordained ritual and with retinues of officials and priests. They wore diadems and sumptuous ornaments. All this represented not a naïve fondness for luxury, but symbolic representations of their dignity as sovereigns. The emperor is exalted in Byzantine churches because he was considered Christ's legate on earth. He bears his offerings to God, as Justinian does with Empress Theodora in the Ravenna mosaics, as a gesture of humility and of gratitude. For he reigns over his subjects just as God the All-Powerful reigns above the world to which He came to redeem it from perdition.

Everything in Byzantine art is thus formalistic, with ranks assigned to the several personages, and the gestures reproduced in the mosaics are stylized. It is didactic, as is much early art: the art in these churches was considered a means of enlightening the masses, of imparting a message to them. It is, above all else, symbolic: the cupola is the form best suited to it, because it recalls the starry heavens; paradise is in the middle zone, the earth down below. Until the fifth century, the priest used to offer the sacrifice of the Mass facing the congregation, not (as became the universal practice later) turning away from it and facing the east. The entrance of churches was then at the eastern end and the whole apse faced west.

The Byzantine interior appears dark to those who are accustomed to the flood of light of Gothic churches, with the ogives lightening their walls and the brightness of stained glass illuminating the interiors. But the mosaics made up for the darkness and gave the Byzantine basilicas a scintillating mobility, a refulgent luminousness which was designed to dazzle the worshipers then and which still dazzles us today. Mosaic, that hard, rebellious, almost intractable material, took on suppleness and variety at the hands of the Byzantine craftsmen. Only in sculpture is Byzantine art decidedly unequal to the Romanesque or Gothic cathedrals. Sculpture had been the triumphant achievement of the Greeks; it had invested their pagan gods with resplendent beauty. But the early Byzantine artists did not strive to emulate, much less surpass, the Greeks, for to them it appeared unholy to chisel statues of God or of His Son; those statues might have been too close to the masterpieces of polytheism. And in any case the Byzantines would never have equaled the sculptures of the Greeks. Moreover, Byzantine churches did not stress the exterior as did the earlier Parthenon or the later Autun, Vézelay or Amiens; their builders preferred relative poverty on the exterior in order to enhance the glory and splendor inside.

The delicate tesserae of glass, paste and mother of pearl on the walls, the cubes of colored stone on the floor flood the interior of St. Sophia with a light which addresses itself to the spirit rather than to the senses. Plotinus, the philosopher who inspired much of Byzantine thought, had pronounced: "No soul could contemplate beauty without being beautiful." Psellus, who lived in the eleventh century and is the most highly praised philosopher of Byzantium, likewise stressed the search for spiritual light behind and beyond the splendor of plastic and pictorial art. The famous Platonic lines of Shelley mourning Adonais aptly convey the character of Byzantine art which refused the weight of matter and the realistic imitation of our earthly abode, but aims at an airiness and a radiance which reveal the truly real world beyond our own:

> "Life, like a dome of many-coloured glass,
> Stains the white radiance of eternity."

That other world of eternity was man's true abode in Byzantine theology; the sumptuousness and even the garishness of Byzantine decoration were considered fully justified as a way of suggesting paradise and the transference of the earth into heaven. Greek art of the age of Phidias provided fuller satisfaction to the intellect and man was idealized, ranked almost with the gods created in his image. The divine, rather than the mortal, rules supreme in Byzantine art; still, the worshiper in the churches drew close to this aura of majesty and did not find forbidding even the portrayal of a stern God facing him with large, watchful eyes.

Indeed, two great inspirers of Byzantine art, the sovereigns whose images at San Vitale have impressed posterity more than any other Byzantine figures, Justinian and Theodora, were human personages—all too human —rendered solemn and august by masters of mosaic. For us they are the most fascinating individuals in the whole range of Byzantine history. The Emperor Justinian, who came to rule over a vast territory and to vanquish the heretics, rose from humble origins. The Empress Theodora was closely associated with him in his imperial rule; the grant of power to women, which had not been a common practice in Greece or Rome, was a characteristic of Byzantine civilization. The emperor did not select Theodora as his empress on any ground of noble birth or impressive ancestry; he did so simply for her charm and her brain. Her ascent to the most glorious throne of Christendom ranks among the startling romances of ancient history.

Theodora probably came from Syria, although certain writers suggest Cyprus, the island of Aphrodite. Her father became a caretaker of bears at the amphitheatre of Constantinople. He died early, leaving a wife and several daughters. The widow, dependent on the benevolence of the crowds at the Hippodrome, soon realized to what use she could put the promising loveliness of her daughter. Theodora became a professional dancer and then a prostitute. After a stay in Alexandria, she turned to a sterner notion of Christianity and attracted the attention of Justinian, then forty and a widower. For twenty-one years she reigned with him, displaying more wisdom and energy than he. She saved his throne during the riots of January 532. While he insisted upon looking back toward the former grandeur of Rome, then sadly fallen, she understood more clearly the advantages of their Eastern dominion. Procopius, Justinian's historian, left secret notes on the empress which indict her savagely as venal, unfaithful, calculating. Gibbon, not usually lenient, seems closer to truth when he hints, in his "Decline and Fall," that her licentious youth had led her to value chastity and the majesty of kingship all the more. "Although she might be saturated with love, yet some applause is due to the firmness of a mind which could sacrifice pleasure and habit to the stronger sense of duty or interest."

Much to her grief, Theodora bore no son to pursue Justinian's achievement. She died on June 29, 548, and her state funeral, ordained by the emperor, was like an apotheosis. To many a visitor to Constantinople and an admirer of Ravenna, she symbolizes the humanity, the dramatic and living background of Byzantine art, which strove so mightily for the serenity and stability of the divine, endeavored to deny the law of change and was engulfed in the shipwreck of time only after a thousand years. In Yeats' words, it sings to us today as it once did:

"To lords and ladies of Byzantium
Of what is past, or passing, or to come."

CHURCH OF THE SANCTA SOPHIA

ISTANBUL

The Emperor Constantine may well be credited with the third place, next to Christ and St. Paul, among the founders of Christianity. Few rulers have had a more far-reaching and enduring effect on history. Born in what is today a part of Yugoslavia, the illegitimate son of Constantius I and of a woman of low birth, he was sent to his father's court as a child. He was a shrewd observer of the dark political intrigues around him. He also studied the art of war and fought under the famed general Galerius on the Danube, at a time when both the Eastern and the Western regions of the once invincible Roman empire were incessantly harassed by Germanic and Slavic hordes, by Persian and Dacian foes farther east. Constantine then joined his father on the English Channel. When Constantius died in the English city which is at present York, the son maneuvered patiently and skillfully in order to be acclaimed emperor by the troops. He had rivals to overcome, the chief of them being Maxentius in Italy. Constantine defeated Maxentius on the Tiber River, and then conquered Rome. He considered that he owed that fateful victory to a vision of the flaming cross which appeared to him at mid-day. On the cross he read the Greek words: "By this conquer."

That vision, and the emperor's subsequent conversion, determined the destiny of Christianity. Through his Edict of Milan in 313 A.D., Constantine secured for the new faith, until then persecuted, full admission throughout the empire. He assumed sovereignty over both East and West and took an active interest in religious affairs. He saw in that a means of strengthening his power and of preventing dissentions over matters of theology. He presided over the great Council of Nicaea in 325, which condemned Arianism as a heresy. The year before, he had selected the city of Byzantium, a Greek settlement on the Bosporus, advantageously located where the Golden Horn and the Sea of Marmara join, as the seat of the Eastern Empire.

In 326, Constantine decided to move the seat of all of the empire from Rome farther to the East, where it would be less exposed to the inroads of the barbarians. Thanks to its legacy of Hellenic culture, this region in what is now Turkey had retained more refined artistic traditions than the West. It was also less wedded to the gods and rites of paganism than were the Roman officials. In 330, the new capital at Byzantium, renamed Constantinople, "the city of Constantine" (its present name, Istanbul, is also of Greek origin and means "toward the city"), was dedicated to the Virgin.

Soon after, just before he died at Nicomedia in a battle against the Persians, Constantine received baptism. He had ridden on the wave of the future more securely than had many a more profound and more imaginative

MONUMENT ON THE BOSPORUS. Sancta Sophia in Istanbul is the supreme expression of Byzantine art. Constructed by the Emperor Justinian, it was a Christian church for its first 916 years. Then, after the Turkish conquest of 1453, it became a Moslem mosque. The four slim minarets were added to it and its Christian mosaics were plastered over at that time. Since 1935 it has been a museum of Roman and Byzantine antiquities and some of its old mosaics are once again on view.

statesman.   He had understood the value of art and he had molded history.   Better than the shortsighted philosophers of his empire, he had realized that polytheism had become out of date—and out of favor with the women, the poor and the underprivileged.   He had perceived what boundless spiritual and material benefits might accrue to his vast dominion from the adoption of Christianity as the state religion.

In the two hundred years that followed Constantine's death, Byzantine culture turned even more sharply away from Rome to assume a definitely Greek character.   The Byzantine civilization, less pragmatic than the Roman, displayed a fondness for theoretical speculations and a taste for subtleties of the mind that were worthy of the interlocutors in Plato's dialogues.   Moderns often forget how close ancient Greece had always been to Asia Minor, commercially and intellectually.   There was much irrationalism in the culture to which we owe the Parthenon, the history of Thucydides and the logic of Aristotle—and Byzantium was the heir to Athens.   But Byzantium was even closer to the Asian continent than Greece was, and Asia was the birthplace of all great religions: Judaism, Christianity, Islam, and the cults of Buddha, Zoroaster, Mithra.   It was left to Europe to transform through Hellenic thought and Roman organization at least one of those faiths.

From 527 to 565 A.D., Constantinople was fortunate in being ruled by another great figure, Justinian. A Macedonian of lowly birth, he pursued lofty conceptions.   Unlike those who had gone before him, he tended to look toward the past greatness of Rome rather than to the past splendors of Greece.   He codified the Roman laws into a whole which now goes by his name, for which achievement Dante granted him a place in his Paradise. "Through the will of God, the first love," Dante has him declare proudly, "I excised from the laws what in them was superfluous and vain." Justinian fought valiantly but unsuccessfully to recover for the empire Africa and the Italian peninsula which had been seized by Germanic invaders.   He mistrusted the disquisitions of philosophers who had lost touch with reality and delighted in imaginary pseudo-problems; among other things, he closed the schools of Athens.   But he favored builders and artists who, in Ravenna and elsewhere, rewarded him by bestowing immortality upon him.   Before his death Constantine had built a basilica (it may thus be called although it was not one technically) in Constantinople.   It was destroyed by fire in 532.   It is to Justinian that we owe the present basilica of Sancta Sophia, reconstructed on the same site; it is one of the most original structures in architectural history.

The early Christian basilicas had been the successors to the secular architecture of Rome, rather than to the ancient temples (where the worshipers did not enter and so the buildings could be small).   In the Greek temples,

24

the greatest care was lavished on the exterior—on the friezes, metopes, statues and marble columns. Such was not the case in Byzantine architecture. The builders of the Byzantine churches were inspired instead by such edifices as the Baths of Caracalla. The Baths date from the beginning of the third century A.D., and even today few of the ruins of classical antiquity produce such an overpowering impression upon the beholder. Nature and art blend at Caracalla to compose one of the most romantic of all landscapes; there innumerable poets and artists have meditated on the fall of empires and on the melancholy grandeur of ruins. Percy Bysshe Shelley wrote most of his "Prometheus Unbound" there. In the preface to that drama Shelley describes the tempestuous loveliness of the site: "the mountainous ruins of the Baths of Caracalla, among the flowery glades and thickets of odoriferous blossoming trees, which are extended in ever winding labyrinth upon its immense platforms and dizzy arches suspended in the air."

In those gigantic Baths, some of the principles that were to guide Byzantine architecture had already been discovered and applied. The builders of Sancta Sophia refined upon and multiplied those principles. Their achievement was unique: they added both greater stability to the construction and more audacity to the scheme.

PORTRAIT OF AN EMPEROR. Constantine IX appears in a mosaic in a gallery of Sancta Sophia. He ruled the Roman Empire from 1042 until 1055, wisely while his wife the Empress Zoë lived, but not very well after she died in 1050. He allowed his army to disintegrate and lost vast areas of his realms in Europe.

As it happened, the country from which materials for the building were drawn was richer in stone than in timber. Thus it was possible to experiment more freely with vaults. The two architects Justinian employed were Anthemius of Tralles and Isidorus of Miletus. Coming from Asia Minor, they were familiar with the achievements of Syrian builders, who had been boldly experimental. Not only were the Sancta Sophia architects expert engineers with a thorough training in mathematics, they were also artists with an eye to effects of beauty. They studied the works of their predecessors, especially, it may be surmised, the huge cistern built by Constantine in the Byzantine metropolis, and various structures in which pyramidal blocks were utilized as capitals. They also had to make their structure as nearly fireproof as possible, to protect it against the vandalism which twice had destroyed earlier churches of Sancta Sophia by fire.

Those fires had been set by mobs of the townspeople who were rioting over theological questions—specifically over the cult of images or the exclusively divine nature of Christ. In Justinian's time, religious disputes could stir more violent emotions than political feuds do in our own day. Indeed, Byzantine crowds were highly emotional at all times. Among other things they could be inflamed by worldly passions, such as today move the fanatics of Spanish bullfights and of other sports events. Near the august and semi-mystical splendor of Sancta Sophia was the famed Hippodrome, where partisan crowds were aroused to a furious pitch of emotion when hailing their champions. The Empress Theodora's fortune began on that race course and many a riot originating there shook the throne of Byzantine emperors.

To help construct his great church, Justinian gathered, in addition to his architects, the finest artistic talent available in his empire and the ablest mathematical minds of Asia Minor, for the problems to be solved were mathematical as well as esthetic. They required competence in trigonometry, in the technique of vaults and pendentives on which to rest a cupola. These scientists were not rigid functionalists in architecture; they valued decoration as an essential element of beauty.

The construction of Sancta Sophia was furthered by the fact that it took place from 532 to 537, a period when Justinian's power stood at its peak. An able general in his service, Belisarius, perhaps one of the greatest commanders in military annals, had momentarily rid Byzantium of the barbarian tribes whose inroads had so long been a nightmare. For the construction of the new church tributes could be, and were, levied far and wide. The inhabitants of dwellings which had to make way for the enormous edifice were dislodged. Monuments standing in Italy, Greece and Asia were plundered to enrich the new building. Emissaries were dispatched to the marble quarries which had provided the Greeks with their finest materials: to continental Greece, to such islands as Marmara (the name means "marble") and others from which, centuries later, such masterpieces as the Venus of Milo and the Victory of Samothrace were to be unearthed.

The most admired of the Athenian shrines, the Parthenon, was a temple of Athena, the goddess of wisdom and of reason. She stood as a symbol of perfection and of the intellectual achievements which in the fifth century B.C. had laid the foundations of science, philosophy and ethics, and had established the canons of Western beauty. The stupendous church planned by Justinian was also to be consecrated to wisdom, but it was to be divine rather than human wisdom. "There is no beauty without measure," Plato had declared in his "Timaeus." Aristotle's "Poetics" had echoed the same conviction that order is the soul of beauty. The Byzantines disagreed. The chief influence on Byzantine art was Plotinus, an Egyptian-born romantic of the ancient world, who in the third century A.D. had stressed the quest for the unfinished rather than the serene contentment of perfect proportions and completion. A certain note which had not been altogether unheard among the Greeks (it strikes us in Euripides and in the most moving reliefs in Athens) becomes much more apparent in Byzantine art: a note of disquietude and longing.

The most arresting features of Sancta Sophia are its immense proportions, and its rich decoration of mosaics. It has a vault which is the most astonishing ever devised by man. Despite the lavishness of the ornamentation the structure gives an impression of restraint. A unified view of this world and of the next is embodied in the church. To the Byzantine mind, as a Greek patriarch put it, "a church was the earthly sky in which God of the Heavens above lives and moves." Its purpose—unlike that of the pagan temples—was to invite the faithful inside; hence its size and its decoration.

Sancta Sophia is entered through nine gates and a double narthex or antechamber. The building is approximately 285 feet long and 216 feet wide. The cupola, redone in 562 after an even more audacious one had collapsed four years earlier, towers more than 160 feet high—higher than the Pantheon in Rome, even higher than the unfinished cathedral of Beauvais, which at 145 feet is the most ambitious of the Gothic shrines. The diameter of the Sancta Sophia dome is 105 feet. The challenge to architects was to adapt the circle of the cupola to the square supporting it. This was achieved through the use of the rounded triangles called pendentives. Over

the upper part of a square—or hexagon or octagon—segments of a spherical surface were adjusted so as to make a circular support for the dome. The Romans had grappled with that architectural problem too. In the course of doing so they may have borrowed the technique of the vault as it had already been developed in Syria, in Egypt and among the Etruscans. But beside Sancta Sophia the Roman buildings seem shrunken, too neatly symmetrical, too rigid in their alignment of columns. Sancta Sophia affords an altogether new suggestion of space. There is no monotony in the pillars and the arches. The longitudinal axis heightens the impression of both length and depth. The vision of the visitor is directed toward the cupola above and to the altar where the sacrifice of the Mass used to be celebrated. God's magnitude and man's insignificance are here contrasted.

The contemporaries of Justinian were loud in their admiration of the sumptuousness of the decoration. Unfortunately, only a few of the mosaics which covered the walls have survived, and those have had to undergo restoration. These luminous mosaics were reflected in the great quantities of marble that were used in the interior.

In the eighth and ninth centuries, following the erection of Sancta Sophia, there occurred the long, fierce War of the Iconoclasts. The popular worship of icons had reached extravagant proportions in Byzantium. It invested the priests and the sellers of relics with excessive power over the superstitious and fearful mob. The imperial power and the Church opposed this practice. A council declared that the supernatural could not be represented by mortals. The iconoclasts—literally "breakers of idols"—set out to destroy the icons. But iconoclasm could not prevail. To Byzantine Platonists, the images were the shadows of higher essences, and artistically portrayed beauty was the envelope of the soul. A new council, held at Nicaea in 787, recommended that art serve as a royal road to faith and suggested that pictures could guide the believer better than preaching. "Things seen are mightier than things heard," the pagan poet Horace had once said.

The architecture and the mosaics of Constantinople radiated their influence to the West (as in Venice, Aix-la-Chapelle and Périgueux) as well as to the East. It is reported that Russian envoys to the Byzantine capital in the tenth century were so impressed by Sancta Sophia that they persuaded their sovereign Vladimir, Duke of Kiev, to adopt the Christian Orthodox faith as the religion of the state. In our own time, Western men—notably the poet W.B. Yeats—have hailed the Byzantine capital as a symbol of the marriage of the legacy of paganism with Christianity, of the mysticism and yearning of the East with the more empirical and rational wisdom of the West.

THE BLESSING. Christ *(opposite page)* has returned to earth and blesses the faithful against a golden field suggesting the light of the faith. This is the central figure in the rediscovered mosaic which is shown in part on page 30.

THE WITNESS. A representation of St. John, praying *(right)*, stands by the figure of Christ, a witness to Him who said: "I am the light of the world; he that followeth me shall not walk in darkness, but shall have the light of life."

SAN VITALE * SANT'APOLLINARE NUOVO SANT'APOLLINARE IN CLASSE

RAVENNA

Ravenna, once a Roman metropolis in the western Mediterranean, and a treasure house of sumptuous decoration, has experienced the strangest fate of any Italian city. While Rome rose to new glory under Popes who rivaled emperors in power and exacted submission from temporal rulers; while bustling Venice, Genoa, Florence and Siena vied with one another in profitable commercial activity and in ushering in the Renaissance, Ravenna lay desolate among her marshes. Nineteenth-century travelers, particularly those enamored of ruins, were fond of carrying their own solitary melancholy to the slumbering city. "A town more forlorn, more sadly fallen from its earlier glory, could hardly be imagined," wrote Hippolyte Taine in the 1860's.

Before interest in the haughty splendor of Byzantine art was revived late in the nineteenth century, most travelers who visited Ravenna did so to search for the shades of two poets, Dante and Byron. When he was banished from his native Florence, Dante was given shelter by the governor of Ravenna, a member of the same family as Francesca da Rimini, who was immortalized by the poet in the fifth canto of the "Inferno." It was in Ravenna that Dante completed the cantos of the "Paradiso," and it was there that he died, on September 14, 1321.

In the twenty-eighth canto of the "Purgatory" he located in the forest of pines of Chiassi, near Ravenna, his encounter with Matilda, who was to lead him to Paradise and to the famous vision of Beatrice with flowers around her. Here Dante compared the whisper of the leaves and the chirping of birds at dawn in those fragrant meadows to the breeze which swings the branches "in the pine grove on the shore of Chiassi, when Eolus sets the southern wind free." A monument to the father of Italian poetry stands in the city of Ravenna.

As for Byron, he went to Ravenna in 1819 in pursuit of young Teresa Guiccioli, who was then his infatuation, and there he began work on a poem entitled "The Prophecy of Dante." He lived on a floor of the palace of Count Guiccioli, which he audaciously rented from the husband of the beauty who was his current muse.

Nowhere has early Christian art survived in such a complete and perfect state as in Ravenna; the city has been called the Italo-Byzantine Pompeii for that reason. Lying on the Adriatic Sea, it was a commercial crossroads where travelers from the Germanic world across the Alps met with those who had come from the East and from African shores. Protected on one side by the sea, the city was guarded on the other by forests, marshes and lagoons. During the fifth and fourth centuries B.C., when the Gauls repeatedly invaded northern Italy and the plain of the Po from the west, Ravenna remained impregnable. The city again proved to be impregnable and went unharmed by Hannibal's forces in 218 B.C., when the Carthaginian chief posed such a dire threat to the Romans.

WALLS OF WONDER. Just inside the entrance arches of San Vitale with their medallion portraits of the Apostles, a second-story gallery blazes with brilliantly colored mosaics of scenes from the lives of Abel, Moses, Melchizedek and others.

A GEOMETRIC CHURCH. The basic structure of San Vitale is an octagon topped by a smaller octagon and dome. It was built during the reign of Emperor Justinian and his wife Theodora, the same pair of Roman rulers who built Sancta Sophia.

The geographer Strabo praised the city's location, on canals which were washed at high tide by sea water, so that the sewage was carried off; the air of Ravenna was considered so pure that gladiators were sent there to be trained. Lying close to the main arteries built by the Romans, the Via Flaminia and the Via Aemilia, Ravenna held the gateway between central Italy and the Po. Even the inscriptions on coins of the period designated it as a fortunate city: "Ravenna Felix." Caesar added to its fame in history when, in 50 B.C., he selected it as his headquarters while he negotiated with the Roman Senate just before he crossed that small, but since famous, river which flows nearby, the Rubicon. Later, Augustus, who had learned the value of sea power during his struggles with Mark Antony, established Ravenna as the home port of one of the two fleets he created. The city enjoyed prosperity in the early centuries of the Christian era. At that time it seems to have suffered only one inconvenience—a dearth of drinking water. Epigrams of the poet Martial describe it as a place where it was easier and cheaper to procure wine than water.

Christianity was brought to Ravenna, according to a legendary tradition, by Apollinaris, a churchman reported to have been a disciple of St. Peter. He had come, it seems, from Syria and suffered for his faith, and his

THE PROCESSION OF THE BLESSED. Two walls in the nave of Sant'Apollinare Nuovo are ornamented with processions. Male saints, led by St. Martin, are shown at the right approaching the Redeemer Who is seated on His throne attended by angels. Female saints, not shown here, approach from the left. Over each saint is his name and although some died young and others old or middle-aged, in the mural they all appear young to show the equality of souls.

relics were long worshiped near Ravenna, in the church at the nearby port of Classis which bears his name: Sant' Apollinare in Classe. By the early years of the sixth century after Christ, barbarian invasions had laid much of northern Italy waste; the administration had broken down; roads and canals were poorly maintained. The frontiers of the Roman world had been breached on all sides by the Vandals, the Lombards, the Visigoths and the Ostrogoths. During this period Ravenna provided a natural barrier against those invaders who, unlike the Normans or the Saracens, had to come by land because they had no skill as navigators. In the fifth century the Emperor Honorius fled Milan as the invader Alaric approached and sought refuge in the harbor of Ravenna. Gibbon has accused Honorius of being "distinguished above his subjects by the preëminence of fear as well as of rank." But retreat, if unheroic, offered the only wise course. It has also been argued that it was only thanks to the flight of Honorius to Ravenna that the new empire which arose to replace the defunct Roman regime was Christian and not heathen. Alaric, bypassing Ravenna, seized and pillaged Rome in the year 409.

It is to Honorius' sister, Galla Placidia, the daughter of the renowned Theodosius I, that we owe many of the most splendid buildings of Ravenna. She had a colorful, adventurous and full life. To begin with, Galla

IMPERIAL POMP AND SPLENDOR. On the right wall of the choir in San Vitale is the celebrated mosaic below, showing the Emperor Justinian coming to church bearing offerings. The emperor is identifiable by his crown and halo. Standing to his left is the Archbishop Maximian. The personage in the rear between the emperor and the bishop is believed to be the banker Julian who was in charge of financing the construction of the church. On the wall opposite this mosaic is another showing Justinian's wife, the Empress Theodora, also attended by dignitaries.

Placidia was among the captives taken hostage by Alaric. The barbarian chief seems to have treated her courteously, but he soon died in southern Italy. His successor was a puzzling warrior, Ataulfus, who had set out to ravage Italy, to obliterate the very name of Rome and to establish the empire of his people, the Visigoths, wherever the Eternal City had once held dominion. But he soon realized that it was not enough to conquer; it was also necessary to maintain law and order, and thus he became, so the historian Orosius tells us, an admirer and upholder of the Roman Empire. Partly for political motives and partly, it appears, because he became enamored of captive Galla Placidia's civilized grace, he married her at Narbonne in 414. Unfortunately, Ataulfus was murdered soon after his wedding, and his widow was sold—perhaps "traded back" would be a kinder expression—to her brother Honorius for 600,000 measures of wheat. Honorius then gave her in marriage to Constantius, who shared the throne with him. The poor woman suffered other tribulations soon after. Constantius died, and she had to seek refuge in Constantinople, where she had spent the early years of her life. She finally returned to Ravenna at the death of Honorius. It is said that she began her career as a builder of churches because of that trip. As she was sailing back to Ravenna in 424 A.D., her ship was tossed about in a gigantic storm. She thereupon vowed to St. John the Evangelist that if she was spared by the elements she would build him a splendid church. The legend adds that a luminous face appeared and soothed the furious waves. She was true to her vow, but the church which she subsequently erected to John the Evangelist no longer exists in its original condition. However, remnants of that structure are preserved in the present church of St. John the Evangelist, which was built some centuries later.

Galla Placidia governed the western empire for a quarter century as regent for her young son, Valentinian III, and in this period she had many rich edifices built.

The present church of St. John the Evangelist is a bold but simple structure, with a polygonal apse adorned with seven windows. Inside, rows of slender columns separate the two lateral aisles from the nave. A square, slender campanile, topped by a pointed spire, was built outside. An inscription relates that its bells were cast in 1208. Their sound is unusually mournful, and a legend grew up to explain this: The German who cast the bells had come to live and work under the sunny skies of Italy in order to cure the melancholy of his lovelorn daughter. The girl pretended to be happy in Italy, but only so as not to grieve her father. At night, she went into her father's shop and wept; her tears, dripping into the molten bronze, gave the bells of St. John's their mournful tone.

MOSAIC OF THE MEADOWS. The birds, flowers and trees of the peaceful country landscape shown on the opposite page, make up part of a mosaic in the church of Sant'Apollinare in Classe. The entire mosaic is an attempt to evoke by subtle and almost mysterious blends of colors and spaces a vision of the Transfiguration of Christ.

The Mausoleum of Galla Placidia is the oldest as well as the most delicately harmonious of the structures that make Ravenna the capital of early Christian art. It has been praised by a great historian of Byzantine art, Charles Diehl, as "perhaps the most exquisite monument left by Christian art." It was built around 420-425 A.D. Despite its name, it is unlikely that Galla Placidia was actually buried there. Her remains probably lie in St. Peter's in Rome. The mausoleum that bears her name is a small structure. Its walls, made of brick, strike the onlooker as modest and bare. A square tower with four slanting roofs hides the handsome cupola, which was built with amphoras ingeniously inserted into one another, as had been the custom with the Romans. This architectural device resulted in a much lighter structure than could otherwise have been the case. Blind arches constitute a decorative motif which breaks the monotony of the plain walls.

From the outside, the mausoleum, though light and graceful, does not give an impression of wealth; indeed, it seems modest, almost poor. The interior is in sharp contrast. The visitor who enters the small building is overpowered by the magnificence of the mosaics. On the floor there are three sarcophagi, probably laid there at a later period. The side walls and the ceiling scintillate with color. At the center of the cupola, the Cross radiates its mystical light. Two figures of Apostles, clad in white robes, their right arms extended, point to the symbol of the Crucifixion and to the dove of the Holy Spirit. The figures of St. Paul and St. Peter display a dramatic force which anticipates Giotto and Masaccio. Close to the starry sky in which the Cross shines are the traditional symbols of the four evangelists, with the golden eagle of St. John especially impressive. This symbolism, later employed in many a cathedral, comes from the verses in the Book of Revelation in which the visionary St. John tells of seeing four creatures—one, which looked like a lion, standing for Matthew; another, resembling a calf, for Mark; a third in the form of a man (Luke) and, last, an eagle flying (John). Various other objects—fruit, leaves, a fawn, two doves poised near a fountain and its bowl—further enhance the naturalness and the graceful naïveté of the scene.

Even more touching is the mosaic of the Good Shepherd and His flock, on the tympanum above the entrance. No masterpiece comparable to this one has come down to us from fifth-century Christian art. The colors used for the figures and background on the tympanum are soft and ingeniously shaded. The Shepherd is stylized, with majesty blending with simplicity in His expression. He is clothed in a long golden tunic over which is draped a red coat. He is seated, holding a golden cross, and benignly watches His flock. Here Christ

has the gentle dignity and grace with which the master sculptors of ancient Greece might have represented an Apollo or an Orpheus. His long hair falls over His shoulders; His cheeks and forehead are slightly tinted with blue.

Elsewhere in the mosaics, St. Lawrence is masterfully portrayed: he carries a cross over his right shoulder; he holds a book in his left hand. On the opposite side, facing the saint, is a small open cabinet, and four books representing the four Gospels rest on the shelves. In the middle is the grill, with lambent red flames, on which St. Lawrence was martyred. Elsewhere, in another semicircular niche, amid intricate traceries of long grasses and plants, two stags drink from a pond. They graphically and charmingly recall the lesson of Psalm XLI—that the soul's thirst for God is like that of the hart which quenches his thirst with clear water.

A second name is everywhere present in Ravenna: that of Theodoric (493-526), a barbarian sovereign who, in his youth, had spent some time in Constantinople and was a staunch admirer of the ancients. He built lavishly. To him we owe the church of Sant' Apollinare Nuovo. After Belisarius, the able general of the Byzantine emperor Justinian, defeated the Ostrogoths and reconquered Ravenna, Justinian and his empress ordered the completion of San Vitale and of Sant' Apollinare in Classe, which had been begun earlier. Ravenna was then the metropolis of the western part of the Byzantine empire, or exarchate, as it was called. (The Greek name means commander-ship: a delegate of the Byzantine emperor governed there.)

San Vitale was planned as early as 527 by the finance minister of the exarchate, and dedicated in 547 by Archbishop Maximian. It owes little to the influence of Sancta Sophia in Constantinople; San Lorenzo Maggiore in Milan, which dates from the late fourth century, might better be considered its predecessor.

A surprising unity was achieved by the builder of San Vitale out of diverse elements, both Western and Eastern. The simplicity of the plan is as admirable as any in later Romanesque churches. The church is an octagon. In each of the eight sections of the wall is an elegant pilaster to provide support for the cupola. The structure is massive and concentric, recalling a fortress; yet it rises boldly and with a kind of animation. While less impressive in size than the most famous of the circular buildings which preceded it, Agrippa's Pantheon in Rome, it is more delicate and purer in its total architectural effect.

The interior is unequaled in the magnificence of the play of light and shade along its apse and its two-storied arcades. In all of Byzantine art, the mosaics of San Vitale rank among the gayest and most eloquent. Among the finest are the two angels over the entrance of the apse, holding a sphere in the center of which is

44

written the first letter of the Greek alphabet, depicting the theme that in the beginning was the Word. The eight beams which intersect at the middle of the sphere symbolize Christ's Resurrection eight days after the entrance into Jerusalem. Jerusalem, on the left of the mosaic, stands for Judaism; on the right is Bethlehem, standing for the Christian church.

On the left wall of the presbytery, the mosaics which record the narrative of Abraham are no less admirable. The patriarch is shown first being visited by three angels who announce that a son will be born to him. Then he is seen preparing to sacrifice his son Isaac, but God's hand, emerging from the clouds above some oak branches, intervenes. On the outside border, Moses is depicted listening to God's warnings on Mount Sinai. Higher still, St. Luke and St. John, shown in association with the animals which traditionally symbolize them, appear in a verdant landscape. Elsewhere an even more striking mosaic represents Abel and Melchizedek preparing to make a sacrifice to the Eternal. Abel is seen coming out of his rustic hut with a lamb; Melchizedek walks out of a more imposing building (it has three naves) and offers the Lord a loaf of bread.

On another wall St. Matthew and St. Mark are shown receiving divine inspiration for the writings in which they are to relate the life of Christ. Near Christ, and ready to be crowned by Him, stands San Vitale; Archbishop Ecclesius, who supervised the building of the church of San Vitale, is shown, too—holding in his hand a model of the octagonal structure. Emperor Justinian and Empress Theodora, during whose reign San Vitale was completed, are portrayed in their regal dignity on the side of the apse. The haughty figure of Justinian, holding a plate of bread for the Consecration to symbolize his role as the ruler of the Church, stands beside a representation of the banker who raised funds for the construction of the building and, farther to the right, the Archbishop Maximian. Opposite Justinian is the even more majestic panel of Theodora, with her jeweled necklace and her heavily ornamented headdress, holding the wine chalice for the Eucharistic ritual. (Both mosaics may have been prepared in Constantinople; neither of the two sovereigns seems ever to have set foot in Ravenna.)

Another octagonal structure, the Baptistery of San Giovanni in Fonte, also called the Baptistery of the Orthodox, is a building of marked simplicity outside, but inside it is richly adorned with mosaics of figures and floral motifs in blues, reds and greens. On the dome are represented the Twelve Apostles, each identified by name and endowed with a distinctive personality. In the center, the scene of Christ's baptism is depicted in a curious fashion. Christ, naked, is receiving the baptism from St. John, who stands beside a river. On the opposite side,

THE CARVED CAPITALS. Structure and decoration are so closely entwined in the churches of Ravenna that it becomes impossible to separate them. The capital at San Vitale *(left)* mingles mosaic and carved marble to create a whole that resembles the precise symmetry of heraldry.

A SYMBOLIC PEACOCK. Against a violet disk the lustrous bird *(right)* in San Vitale flourishes its feathers in an irridescent display. It is meant to suggest to the faithful the light and loveliness, the eternal spring and unending enchantment of the world Christians believe after death.

the Jordan river is shown in human form, holding a reed and a cloth to wrap the body of Christ. This personification of the river bears clear traces of pagan origins. This is not surprising, for in Ravenna, East and West, Greek polytheism and the monotheistic tradition inherited from Judaism, exuberance of color and sobriety of architecture—all blended to form a new art.

The mixture of styles and periods is typified by the church of Sant' Apollinare Nuovo. The name was affixed to the structure relatively late; when Theodoric, the Romanized Ostrogoth sovereign, had the building erected, it was intended as a temple of the Arian cult. Arius, an Alexandrian priest of the early fourth century, had aroused tremendous theological controversy by contending that the Son of God was a created being who preceded the creation of the world, but was not identical with the eternal God. His views caused ferocious debates among the theologians and the faithful. In the end, Arius was excommunicated, and Constantine, eager to preserve his empire from dogmatic strife, had the Arian heresy condemned in 325 by the famous Council of Nicaea. The Son was then and there declared to be of the same substance as the Father, neither created nor subordinate. But the Arian doctrine lingered on and it had partisans in Theodoric's Ravenna, which is why Theodoric planned a church for the heretical group.

Sant'Apollinare Nuovo underwent alterations after its original construction. Its high tower in brick, with windows divided into three openings by slim pillars on the two higher floors, dates from the tenth century at the earliest. Its marble portico was erected even later. The shape of the church is that of a basilica. It is preceded by a narthex or outer portico, frequently seen in Byzantine and in Italian architecture. Those who were excluded from entering the church itself because of some penance were allowed into the narthex.

Inside, an impressive effect is achieved by the semicircular apse and by the long rows of arcades, resting on pillars of marked elegance. On the walls, three horizontal strips of mosaics rise to the ceiling. The highest may date from Theodoric's era; the others were completed at a later date. One, showing Lazarus raised from the dead, has a rigidity that gives it a special magnificence. The evocation of the last days of Christ is more graceful. One of the mosaics of this group represents Pilate, washing his hands in a basin handed to him by a servant while he gazes at Christ with a disturbed countenance. Elsewhere, the Redeemer advances, impassive, to Calvary, taller than the man who bears the cross on His left and than the priests who follow. Even one much-restored mosaic, that of Christ surrounded by four angels and holding a sceptre, conveys an inescapable sense of sublime majesty.

48

Better known are the rows of mosaics above the arcades, depicting two solemn processions. One represents the male martyrs and saints, all looking in the direction of Christ. This procession is led by St. Martin, to whom the church was once dedicated. The other is a procession of twenty-two women, virgin martyrs. They are preceded by the three Magi. The women's heads, covered with elegant mitres and surrounded by halos, are slightly bent; their attire glitters with gold and jewels; the draperies of their dress recall the rhythm of ancient statues. It is hard not to be reminded of the Parthenon frieze of the Panathenaea, although the mosaic faces are tenser and lack the sunny naturalness of the Greek.

To the ancient port of Classis, near Ravenna and beyond Caesarea, Byzantine sailors once brought goods, and probably art as well from the other shore of the Adriatic and from the Levant. Here Sant'Apollinare in Classe still stands miraculously preserved from the destruction with which it was threatened by the German retreat from Italy at the end of World War II. Now it is strangely isolated among the fields. The onetime seaport stands on dry land, for the sea has withdrawn. The campanile, built outside the church in the Italian manner, towers above flat countryside. The building was completed by the middle of the sixth century.

The superb basilica of Sant'Apollinare in Classe, like San Vitale, is built of brick. On either side of the basilica is a smaller square structure with an even smaller pentagonal projection at its end. Long, dry grasses and wind-bent trees grow all around. The setting and the architecture are harmonious. Inside, the restrained beauty and the felicitous proportions of the apse make Sant'Apollinare the finest Christian basilica erected before the time of the Romanesque builders. The simplicity of the church is due in part to the losses it suffered through the ages. Its floor and its walls used to be covered with marble; today, only the marble of the columns remains.

The mosaics rank among the most glorious in Christendom. Among them are pictures of St. Mark and St. Luke, the serene and majestic Archangel Michael, and Moses and Elijah. Most remarkable, however, are those showing the Transfiguration of Christ. Six lambs emerge right and left from the two cities symbolizing the Old and the New Law, Jerusalem and Bethlehem. In the center of the starry firmament on the vault is a bejewelled cross with the first and the last letters of the Greek alphabet, Alpha and Omega, at the two ends, along with the five letters which stood for "Jesus Christ, Son of God, Savior" (and which spelled the Greek word for "fish"). At the center of the cross is the head of Christ, and on either side are three sheep standing for the disciples Peter, James and John, who witnessed the Transfiguration. St. Apollinaris raises his hands for an invocation.

The Byzantine art of Ravenna reached a summit of religious, architectural and decorative greatness. It united several distinctive elements which are seldom found together in later eras of Christian art. It is essentially an imperial and official art, displaying the emperor and the empress among state officials, the bishops and other members of their court. It was an art that was at the service of the state while offering lessons of dogma to the faithful. There was another side to Byzantine culture that addressed itself to tradesmen, artisans, peasants and the lower levels of the ecclesiastical hierarchy; it had a freer folklore and even displayed some realism in the depiction of contemporary life. But it is not present in Ravenna's solemn churches.

The Byzantine artist remains aloof from us; he is impersonal and anonymous and fulfills a function almost like that of a priest performing his ritual. This art is also theocratic; it simultaneously celebrates God and God's vicar on earth, the emperor. God, or Christ the Pantocrator, towers above the Disciples, Prophets, martyrs and saints who surround Him. Their figures tend to be allegorical.

The religious character of this art is very deep, but it has little appeal to the emotions; it strives toward a stern, didactic rendering of such themes as Incarnation and Redemption. But in its decoration and through its unequaled mastery of the medium of the mosaic, the art of Ravenna ranks among the most colorful of all the expressions of religious mysteries ever offered to Christians. The human body is chastely concealed under sumptuous vestments and jewelry. Relief and form are sacrificed to highly felicitous color effects. It is not surprising that the greatest of colorists among painters appeared in Venice, a city close to Ravenna and influenced by Constantinople. If the faces depicted at San Vitale or at Sant'Apollinare Nuovo and in other churches at Ravenna are not illuminated by the smile of the Ionian statues and lack the serene humanity of Doric sculpture, they nevertheless have the capacity to impress us profoundly. They display an exalted conception of the divine. They exemplify the very original relationship established in Byzantine art "between the world of the beholder and the world of the image." The words are those of a learned student of that art, the Austrian Otto Demus. In his volume, "Byzantine Mosaic Decoration," he adds:

"The relationship was certainly closer in Byzantine than it was in Western medieval art . . . the beholder was not kept at a distance from the image; he entered within its aura of sanctity, and the image, in turn, partook of the space in which he moved. He was not so much a 'beholder' as a 'participant.' While it does not aim at illusion, Byzantine religious art abolishes all clear distinction between the world of reality and the world of appearance."

THE GREAT NAVE AT CLASSIS.   Started during the episcopacy of Archbishop Ursicinus (533-536), the Basilica of Sant'Apollinare in Classe, with its great golden cross, remains a profoundly impressive structure even though over the centuries it has lost much of its wealth in marble walls and floor mosaics.   The church was constructed under the general direction of the banker Julian who also financed the building of San Vitale.   The columns, twelve in each row, are made of marble quarried on the shores of the Sea of Marmara and brought to Ravenna. Their capitals are ornamented with stone acanthus leaves so artfully carved that they seem to move to some mysterious wind.   The golden cross, with the head of Christ at its center, floats in a star-filled sky and together with other mosaics near by symbolizes the Transfiguration on the Mount.

ST. MARK'S

VENICE

No city, not even Rome, "the eternal city," or Paris, "la ville lumière," has ever been celebrated so widely as Venice. None has done more to set the imagination of Western man afire. And in all probability, none has disappointed chimerical expectations so often.

The great monument of Venice is St. Mark's, next to St. Sophia the greatest Byzantine edifice in the world. Its beauty surpasses anything erected in the West from the time of Ravenna in the sixth century to the Pisan baptistery in the twelfth. But the religious spirit behind its architecture has more than once been questioned. The sincerity of the fervor which expressed itself through such lavish decoration has been viewed dubiously by many visitors from across the Alps, the Channel and the Atlantic. Mary McCarthy, in a brilliant volume on the "sea-girt city" and its shrines, blending admiration and irony, rightly remarked that Venice holds the strange power to arouse the Philistine who slumbers within the heart of every skeptic. Philippe de Commynes, a fifteenth century French historian who pierced through much sham in politics and in life, was among the first to be carried away by enthusiasm for the fairy-like city. A hundred years later, Montaigne, who amiably practiced suspension of disbelief in the presence of many creeds and prejudices, found that Venice was unequal to what he had been led to expect. Much later, Stendhal also slighted Venice although he was enamored of Milan.

Enough other Frenchmen have paid lavish tribute to the Queen of the Adriatic. The destroyer of the Venetian Republic, Napoleon, lauded the Square of St. Mark's as "the best drawing-room in Europe." All sorts of people have been drawn to the city on the lagoon. Wagner and Robert Browning died there. Marcel Proust yearned through the years of his sickly youth, like the hero of his novel, for a trip to the city of canals. But once there, sheltered by his mother's tender care, he failed to be moved as much as Turner and Ruskin had led him to expect by the Byzantine church. In preference to that oriental vision of Arabian nights, he favored Giotto's frescoes in the little chapel in Padua.

Venice possesses neither the severe charm of Tuscan hill towns nor the resplendence of Rome, with its churches and the tragic grandeur of Michelangelo's Sistine frescoes. It long ago became the mecca of tourists who stroll along its arcades and its shops. They invade St. Mark's in flocks, listen to the descriptions and anecdotes of the guides, and get a glimpse of an oriental world before they rush to take a gondola trip, working their cameras feverishly. Few are those who take time to understand the originality of the great Venetian church. Some historical imagination—the ability to live, in the mind, in another age and another land—is required for a true appreciation of St. Mark's. This church remains unique as the evidence of a magnificent rebirth of civilization at a midpoint between the Byzantine East and Western Europe.

Venice was not erected on the Adriatic lagoons merely to serve as an eccentric showcase. The site was selected out of dire necessity. When the Huns, held in check by the Chinese in the Far East, turned their greed for plunder toward the West, they drove before them a motley mass of Slavs and Germans. These refugee hordes overran the weakening civilizations of Italy. Some Italians sought refuge in the islands of Torcello and Murano, inaccessible to tribes whose strength was entirely bound to the land. Venice thus arose on the lagoons—"Ocean's child, and then his queen," as Shelley called her. As early as the fifth century Theodoric, the Ostrogoth ruler of Ravenna, dispatched emissaries to the Venetians to ask them to provide salt from their marshes. "Live without gold we can, but not without salt," he said. By the eighth century, the Venetians had realized that their calling was to be wedded to the sea: the Pope at that time begged them to assist in recapturing Ravenna from the Lombard invaders. Later Venetian merchants sailed across the Mediterranean Sea and engaged in commerce with the Moslems, in spite of specific Christian prohibitions against such trade.

In 828, two of these merchants got possession of the relics of St. Mark in Alexandria, Egypt. There are various narratives about the relics. One relates that the author of the Second Gospel was the founder of the See of Aquileia, northeast of Venice; one day, while traveling on his evangelizing mission and stopping at one of the Venetian islands, he had been visited in his sleep by an angel who had told him: "Peace to you, Mark Evangelist, your bones will rest in this very spot." A splendid painting by Tintoretto immortalizes the scene. The Venetian merchants thus felt justified in transferring the newly acquired bones of the city's patron saint to their destined burying place. Finding it necessary to dupe the Egyptian authorities, who would not have allowed the precious relics to be taken away, they said that the package carried to their ship on the back of a camel was pork meat. The horrified Moslems, to whom pork was impure, did not investigate further.

The Venetians do not deny that the wealth of their church was accumulated with scant regard for the usual rules of business ethics—and is displayed with even less regard for historical accuracy. For example, tradition holds that an image of the Virgin shipped to Venice had been painted by St. Luke himself; that columns for the great church came from the temple of Solomon; that the effigy of the Savior on the gate of St. Mark's treasury was chiseled in Jerusalem before Christ's death; that the four pillars on each side of the choir were the very same

THE TREASURE OF VENICE. With its cupolas gleaming in the sun and its façade bright with slabs of marble and glass mosaic, sumptuous St. Mark's, its façade often changed and embellished since its construction in the eleventh century, shimmers in the tidal water that has flooded in on the piazza from the nearby Grand Canal. Across the square, one of the finest in Europe, people pick their way on the duck boards.

MEMORIAL TO A HISTORIC DAY. Over the left portal to St. Mark's, called the Portal of St. Alipius, is a mosaic showing the church when the relics of St. Mark the Evangelist arrived from Alexandria. The two bishops in the center carrying the remains into the church are surrounded by the Doge and the Lords of Venice.

that supported Pilate's tribunal when Jesus was brought to His judgment. The church is also credited with having in its possession a thorn from Christ's crown, a finger of Mary Magdalen's hand, the text of St. Mark's gospel written in the Evangelist's own hand.

It was taken to be the duty of every Venetian official and trader to bring back some gift to the religious edifice around which the life of the city revolved. Since funeral processions of defunct doges passed in front of the church (the coffin was raised nine times there, before proceeding to the burial in Sts. Giovanni and Paolo) and since every new doge also had to be acclaimed there by the people, it is not surprising that the church was continually enriched and its front luxuriously adorned.

The church has always been far more than a shrine for worship. It exists in relation to the "piazza"—the only square thus labeled in Venice: others are called "campi." The square is a vast and elegant portico enclosed on one side by St. Mark's. With other churches, such as St. Sophia and San Vitale, exterior appearance counted but little; here it rivals the inside in splendor. To provide a fitting decor for St. Mark's, the square was rearranged; a canal which divided it was removed, as were some buildings.

The present church was built on the site of an earlier edifice, destroyed by fire in 976 during a riot against a tyrannical doge. It was completed in 1094, twenty-five years before the church of St. Front in Périgueux, to which it has similarities. The inspiration for St. Mark's architecture was derived from the Church of the Holy Apostles in Constantinople. The shape is that of a Greek cross, the transept and the nave being of equal length. The architect's identity is shrouded in legend. The most picturesque of the accounts relates that to build the church there arrived from Constantinople a skilled builder, both of whose legs were maimed. This Byzantine architect promised to design the most beautiful church which could possibly be erected, provided a marble statue of himself was placed inside it. After the building was up, however, he was imprudent enough to admit that an even finer church might have been built. The doge, irate, had him sculpted with his two crutches, but biting his finger out of anger at not having been treated fairly by his Venetian master. The statue still stands.

The outward appearance of St. Mark's was brought into harmony with the square only in the early thirteenth century, when the "Procuratie" and their handsome loggias and arcades were completed. The campanile, whose golden angel welcomes the visitor with extended arms, as Proust put it, collapsed in 1902 and was rebuilt exactly as it had stood. The five cupolas at the entrance might easily have appeared heavy and over-ornamented,

IN THE CHURCH OF THE QUEEN OF THE ADRIATIC. The opulence of the years when Venice ruled the seas is seen everywhere in St. Mark's. Few churches are so luxuriously adorned in fine enamels, precious marbles and priceless mosaics, so richly bathed in golds and blues and purples. The crossing of the nave and transept is topped by the cupola of the Resurrection with thirteenth-century mosaics. The choir is separated from the rest of the church by a curtain of red marble. Everything combines to create an air of oriental wealth and splendor.

THE BAPTISM OF THE SAVIOR. The never-changing themes of Christian art flourish on the walls of St. Mark's. This photograph is of a mosaic of Jesus Christ being baptized by John the Baptist. It was ordered by the Doge Andrea Dandolo sometime between 1343 and 1354, in the final flowering of the Byzantine art.

but the fault was avoided through the skill with which the pillars separating those cupolas were mounted with elegant rows of slender columns and with a terrace above. The stone festoons of the arcades are light and graceful, yet not excessively frail. Many a painting by Venetian artists, who were even more intent than the French Impressionists on portraying the changing appearance of their city, has made that view of St. Mark's front popular.

Additions had to be made to the original plan after St. Mark's square was redone as a setting for the church. The early cupolas, which are depicted in a mosaic of the Miracle of the Relics, on the right arm of the transept, were made taller through a wooden structure covered with gilt lead that was skillfully placed over them. The main gates to the building might have appeared too low once the tops of the cupolas were raised, except that pinnacles, pointed Gothic arrows, were added; they harmonize quaintly and felicitously with the Byzantine domes. Ornaments and mosaics provided color and through the richness of their effect compensated for the restricted space that was at the disposal of the architects. The improvements to St. Mark's were completed only in the thirteenth century; at that time the church was joined with the Ducal Palace, and the vista of the Piazetta and the Lagoon was invested with the magnificence which we admire today.

Outside St. Mark's, the winged lion, symbol of the second Evangelist, and the bronze horses have struck the imagination of countless visitors. The horses are among the finest sculptural ensembles that have come down to us from Greece. They have been attributed to the famous sculptor Lysippus. The Romans took them from defeated Greece to adorn Nero's arch, and later the Arch of Trajan. Constantine in turn carried them to the Hippodrome of his Byzantine capital. When the old, energetic Doge Dandolo directed the Fourth Crusade against Constantinople, he won as spoils the islands of Corfu, Zanta and Crete, the Peloponnesus, and St. Sophia—and he also won those splendid bronze horses, which he shipped home to Venice. Doge Dandolo, then an old man, died soon afterward and was buried in St. Sophia.

In 1797, Napoleon Bonaparte, having defeated the Austrians in his swift Italian campaign, threatened to lay Venice waste unless it surrendered. Surrender it did, without a fight. Philosophers and poets alike mourned the extinction of the Venetian Republic. Wordsworth was inspired by the event to compose one of his most perfect sonnets:

"Once did She hold the gorgeous East in fee
And was the safeguard of the West;..."

IN THE GARDEN CF GETHSEMANE. The mosaic representing this episode in the life of Jesus was made in the thirteenth century by an unknown artist. It shows Jesus on the night of His agony reproaching Peter for falling asleep with the others and not keeping watch during the bitter hours while the Lord prayed.

CHRIST IN STONES AND PEARLS. In this detail of the main altar retable in St. Mark's, a Christ dressed in blue and seated before a golden background both blesses and teaches. His halo, throne, book and the frame about Him are studded with pearls and other precious jewels. The whole work, which contains 30 pounds of gold and 260 pounds of silver, was ordered in Constantinople in 976.

Gloomily and sternly, he concluded:

> "Men are we, and must grieve when even the shade
> Of that which once was great is passed away."

Bonaparte planned to adorn his triumphal arch in the Carrousel with the Venetian horses, and he had them crated and sent off to Paris, along with the winged lion. The entire menagerie was returned after his defeat at Waterloo, in 1815. In the course of the lion's travels across the Alps, the precious stones which were the pupils of its eyes disappeared. The Venetians consoled themselves by saying that the proud king of animals was thus spared the sight of its country's woes—that is, Venice's occupation by Austria-Hungary until 1864. The lion and horses have stood unmolested outside St. Mark's since their return from France.

Through the narthex of the church, which filters the bright light outside and mutes the gay sounds of the square, access is gained to the sanctuary itself. There the many marble columns and the three naves lead to the richly adorned semi-circular apse, beyond the jube and its two porphyry pulpits. Reliefs on the balustrade of the choir and the images of the four Evangelists were sculpted in 1570 by Sansovino. The golden cupola, the red marble of the columns, above all, the glittering mosaics give luminous brightness to the otherwise dark interior.

No other Italian mosaics, with the possible exception of those at Monreale and at Cefalù in Sicily, can match those of St. Mark's in expressiveness and variety. Frescoes would not have proved well adapted to a damp maritime climate. Painting was later to enjoy a splendid flowering in Venice and several of the late mosaics of St. Mark's (for example, the Last Judgment above the arch at the entrance, and St. Mark in Ecstasy on the vault of the narthex) were done from designs by Tintoretto and Titian. But the emergence of great painting was probably delayed by the prestige long enjoyed by the art of mosaics. The fifteenth century was an age of Venetian triumph in the arts. St. Mark must have protected the artists of his city, all indefatigable workers; for, as Mary McCarthy has remarked, a strikingly large number of them reached the biblical age of three score years and ten: the three Bellinis, Titian, Tintoretto, Veronese, Lorenzo Lotto, the two Tiepolos and the two Longhis, Guardi and Canaletto. Venice, skilled in the working of glass, excelled in combining those cubes of enamelled glass which made Venetian mosaics more translucent than the Roman mosaics of marble and stone. Unfortunately, only a few of the original mosaics have survived, such as the one depicting the recovery of the body of St. Mark (the

THE LEGEND OF ST. MARK. The remains of the Apostle Mark were, legends say, transported amid many wonders to the church consecrated to him in Venice. In the course of the voyage from Alexandria the apostle *(see below)* suddenly appeared to the pilot and warned him that he was close to land and might run aground. The solemn reception of his bones at St. Mark's is shown at the Portal of Alipius *(page 59)*. But later, after a fire in the church, all traces of them were lost. Then after prayers by the Patriarch, the Doge and all the people of Venice, they were miraculously found again, as the mosaic on the opposite page shows. The mosaics on these pages date from the thirteenth century.

THE CUPOLA OF THE PENTECOST. The first large cupola a visitor encounters after passing the narthex is consecrated to the Pentecost, the seventh Sunday after Easter when the Holy Ghost descended upon the Apostles. In the center is a dove representing the Holy Ghost and from it come rays of grace to the twelve Apostles. The couples represent people awaiting conversion. The whole is bathed in warm gold to suggest the beauties of the hereafter.

so-called "Miracle of the Relics"), in the right transept, and those showing Christ's Passion and Resurrection, on the arch of the cupola inside the church. All of these are from the thirteenth century.

The themes of the St. Mark's mosaics are in part the traditional scenes of Christian art: the Prophets announcing the New Law; the Church, symbolized at the center of the basilica; the Apostles, in the Pentecost cupola, setting out to convert the gentiles; the Church glorified in the arch of Paradise. Various episodes of the Savior's life inspired the artists, among them Jesus being baptized, reproduced here, and Jesus advocating the payment of tribute money to Caesar. The mosaic of the baptism is, in its moving majesty, not unworthy of the great painting on the same theme done in the fifteenth century by Cima da Conegliano. Christ praying in agony on the Mount of Olives that the bitter chalice may be averted from Him anticipates the tragic eloquence of Tintoretto. The mosaic depicting Christ in His youth, with the Virgin in prayer surrounded by thirteen Prophets, each holding the scroll of His prophecy of the New Law, has retained the simplicity of its Byzantine models and added to it a note of tender humanity. The technique of mosaics, handed down from generation to generation, retained naturalness and allowed for fresh innovations. The rich harmony of the colors softened whatever dryness might have resulted from the stress upon design, inevitable in mosaics.

Another group of mosaics portrays scenes from the life of the saint for whose remains the church was erected and adorned as a shrine. The Venetians did not recoil before pious frauds in order to perpetuate the cult that united them. The legends regarding their saint extolled their past and gave them confident faith in the future of their city. When the first church dedicated to St. Mark was destroyed by fire and the body presumably consumed, it was said that the saint's remains had in fact survived in some unknown location, which would be revealed only in answer to fervent prayers imploring divine guidance. The prayers were offered up; just as predicted, so the story goes, from a pillar of the new church first an arm, then the whole body of the saint appeared.

Among the treasures of St. Mark's is a Madonna of great fame, much honored by the Venetians, the Madonna Nicopeia; the name means "the one who brings victory." It is said to be a Byzantine icon captured during the sack of Constantinople under Doge Dandolo. Even if it is but a copy of the Byzantine original, as is likely, its loveliness under its wealth of pearls and stones remains striking. Even more venerated is the Pala d'Oro, a retable of glittering gold and enamel, profusely decorated with diamonds and pearls, raised under columns brought from Istria and the Balkan peninsula. The Pala d'Oro was first ordered in Constantinople by Doge

CUPOLA OF CREATION. The cupola of the narthex is consecrated to creation and original sin. In three concentric circles the Biblical story of the beginnings of the world and its creatures and the temptation and fall of Adam and Eve can be clearly followed. These pictures strongly resemble the miniatures often found in Eastern Bibles and for this reason, among others, are different from many of the other mosaics, which were done under the influence of the West.

Pietro Orseolo in 976, was completed thirty years later and was finally clad in its sumptuous vestment of precious stones only in 1345. Its abundance of riches may somewhat overpower visitors of ascetic taste. But the figure of the Redeemer blessing, surrounded by the Apostles, is among the most arresting sights of St. Mark's.

In every part of the church, Venetian history comes to life, conjuring up the many literary and historical connections which make Venice part of the past of any cultured person. Inside the church, a square of red marble with a white lozenge marks the spot where Frederick Barbarossa reluctantly knelt before proud Pope Alexander III. Both had been brought to Venice by Doge Sebastiano Ziani.

> "St. Mark yet sees his lion where he stood
> Stand, but in mockery of his withered power
> Over the proud place where an Emperor sued."

Thus wrote Byron in the fourth Canto of "Childe Harold," alluding to that historic encounter of July 13, 1177. Within thirty years, the western chiefs of the Fourth Crusade, in dire need of Venetian ships to carry them across the seas and of funds to pay for them, met in the church. Encouraged by the shrewd old Doge, they stormed and shamefully plundered the Christian city of Constantinople for Venice's benefit. The rift between the Eastern and the Western churches and worlds was never to be healed. The weakened East was to fall easy prey to the Turks in the fifteenth century. Constantinople became a Turkish city and St. Sophia a mosque.

It became fashionable, after the Renaissance, to speak condescendingly of Venetian decadence and immorality. It is true that the art of Venice, which heaped up the glitter of gold, onyx and ruby, carried in itself the seeds of its death. Affluent societies do not necessarily maintain for long an energetic culture; the privilege of guiding history passes on from one maritime republic to another: Genoa, Holland, France, Britain were others who knew the hegemony that Venice had long enjoyed. The word "decadence" is unfair to the city which in 1518 gave rise to Tintoretto, Michelangelo's sole Italian rival; which attracted Palladio, one of the great town planners of all time; which erected the bridge of the Rialto and the lovely baroque church of La Salute; which produced in the eighteenth century Giambattista Tiepolo, a painter whose power is often underestimated, Piranesi, an inspired visionary, and Goldoni, one of the few genuine successors to Molière in comedy. To those Venetians and to many who have since been drawn to the sea-girt city, St. Mark's has represented one of the supreme expressions of Christian faith.

VISIONARY DEVOTION

ROMANESQUE CHURCHES

Toward the third year after one thousand, on nearly the whole earth but chiefly in Italy and France, people began to build basilicas. One would have said that the world, shaking off and rejecting its old age, was covering itself with a white mantle of churches. The faithful were then not content with rebuilding cathedrals; they also restored the churches of monasteries and even small village churches." Thus the Benedictine monk Raoul Glaber wrote in a famous passage of his Chronicle. The monk clearly states that many churches had been erected before 1000 A.D., the year assigned by prophecies and by popular fear as the end of the world and the Day of Doom.

We know that art had not been lacking in Carolingian, even in Merovingian, times in France. But there had been a haunting conviction in many minds that the world was growing old and weary. *Mundus senescit*— "the world is growing old"—wrote a clerk in those years. (A similar fatigue would be felt in the literature and culture of the fifteenth century, in the closing years of the nineteenth, and at other times.) It was feared that Christ was to come and judge the dead, who would be brought back to life to account for their sins. He was to be preceded, as the Book of Revelation had announced, by the Antichrist. When the fatal date came and passed without mishap, it is probable that fears were relieved, that gratitude filled many hearts, and that men everywhere set to erecting temples to voice their appreciation of God's forgiveness. Man was convinced that the Creator had mercifully granted His creatures a new compact of alliance.

In that sense, faith raised mountains, or walls, vaults, towers and spires. That faith also endeavored to impart its feeling to others, to teach those who could not or did not read, like the mother of François Villon (as the poet recalled in charming and touching lines). Recent interpretations of medieval art have been overly subtle or overly ambitious. They have tried to establish a close correspondence between scholastic philosophy and medieval architecture. They have attributed to the age of Cluny and the Cistercians, to that of Notre Dame of Paris and of St. Thomas, far more unity than it had in fact. For there were dissenters long before the Reformation. Sermons were preached even then against selfishness, affluence, greed, the levity of women, the disorders of youth.

But the men of the twelfth century had not yet acquired a sense of history and the notion of relativity, or evolved methods to ascertain facts and to sift evidence. Their creativity had its source in their freshness of imagination. To them, any prophecy formulated in the Old Testament must have been fulfilled in the New. The convergence of two stories, one of them often being interpreted symbolically, was tantamount to evidence. Samson and David were prefigurations of Christ. Samson, "eyeless in Gaza" and carrying off the gates of that city, was the antecedent of Christ treading on the gates of Hell. Jonah in the belly of the whale for three days forecast Christ's sojourn in His grave. Goliath, like Satan, was vanquished by David, who prefigured Christ. St. Paul and St. Augustine served as authorities for the doctrine that the New Testament was hidden in the Old and that the Old was unveiled in the New. Such a conviction is expressed over and over again in Romanesque sculpture, in the paintings of the same style, in the stained-glass windows of St. Denis and Chartres later. In this sense, one is justified in saying that these medieval buildings offer a concrete embodiment of the splendor of the Christian faith. These artists did not consciously and clumsily set out to prove the abstract views of Vincent of Beauvais or of St. Thomas. But their sensibility and their imagination were impregnated with Christian faith. Jacques Maritain cogently expressed it in his "Art and Scholasticism": "The builders of cathedrals . . . did not want either to demonstrate the advantages of Christian dogma or to suggest a Christian emotion through some artifice. . . . They believed and, such as they were, they accomplished their work. Their art revealed the truth of God, but without purposely attempting to do so, and precisely because it did not purposely try to do so."

The splendor of medieval buildings was detested by some of the more puritanical contemporaries of Romanesque art, notably of St. Bernard, that eloquent advocate of Cistercian severity. "Vanity of vanities!" he exclaimed, "but folly even more than vanity! The Church is all glittering on her walls, but she is nude in her poor. She covers her stones with gold and leaves her sons without clothing!" (But even St. Bernard, as Etienne Gilson remarked, would never have renounced one luxury: that of speaking and writing with beauty.) There was some excess of ornament in Cluniac abbeys and in the hostels erected by the monks from that wealthy center (one, in the Paris Latin Quarter, serves as a museum). But it was not unreasonable or impious to wish to devote to God the very best and finest that man could buy or devise. The art survives to bear witness to that unconquerable hope.

Architectural technique had naturally to serve as the handmaiden to religious faith. Lessons from ancient Rome, from Byzantine and Moslem civilizations, from the sculptures and designs of strange animals and plants imported from the East were absorbed by Romanesque artists. Vaults became the essential element of these churches, whose wooden framework of carpentry had so often gone up in fire in the past. The walls had to be built thicker and firmer to withstand the pressure of the vault. Apertures were thus few and far between, and light inside the churches was scarce. (Gothic builders, as we shall see, would later go to the other extreme, multiplying openings, stained glass and delicate traceries.) But the severity of Romanesque art seems to us today to express one of the permanent and deep-seated strains in the character of the Spaniards, the Italians of Tuscany, the French who produced the Albigensian heresy, the creed of the Waldenses, John Calvin, Jansenism and Jacobinism. In this architecture, characterized by solidity and honesty, restrained sobriety of ornamentation, firm balance and intellectual order, the people who erected Vézelay and Albi, who sculpted at Moissac and Autun, who painted religious scenes at St. Savin and Tavant evinced the two qualities which characterize the style of St. Bernard, of Calvin, of Pascal, and of Camus in our own day: geometry and passion.

Romanesque was not always the most cherished legacy of the Middle Ages. The romantic era in Western Europe, which had to its credit, among other things, the rediscovery of the Middle Ages, preferred Gothic to Romanesque. But the middle decades of the twentieth century have witnessed some dissatisfaction with the perfection of Notre Dame of Paris, the spires of Strasbourg and of Cologne, the rich ornamentation of the Rouen Cathedral. Our time reserves its warmest admiration for other periods: for archaic Egyptian or Greek art, for pre-Columbian masks, functional architecture, the painting of squares, circles or even parallel lines such as followers of Mondrian, Delaunay and Malevich have favored, a sculpture which is devoid of any reference to man, and Romanesque art, rather than Gothic art and architecture. Nowadays the barest, most massive of Cistercian abbeys in the Romanesque style are often those which appeal most to us. Romanesque sculpture is preferred by many even to the Royal Portal of Chartres and to the "Beau Dieu" of Amiens.

Neither the word Romanesque nor what the word represents is very clearly understood. The English form, "Romanesque," is the most unfelicitous of all. The German language calls it "Romanisch" and used to call it "Old Gothic." "Romanico" is the Italian and Spanish form for the adjective designating that style. They all derived from the French adjective, "roman," which is itself of relatively recent birth. It was coined by two Norman antiquarians in 1818, De Gerville and Le Prévot, to be applied to what then went by the appellation of "Saxon" or "Norman." An archaeologist of some note, Arcisse de Caumont, popularized the word in a volume published in 1824. In the sense that it stresses the similarity between Romanesque art (especially in its use of the vault) and Roman architecture, the term is slightly misleading. The scholarship of later years has taken pains to underline influences other than that of Rome that were exerted on this early medieval architecture.

The area to which it spread is more easily specified: it extended to Spain, Italy, England, Germany (where it lasted longer and impeded the development of the architecture called Gothic, although Gothic had little that was Germanic about it). It flourished most brilliantly in southern, western and central France. There are Romanesque buildings, or details, in Santiago de Compostela and in Catalonia, in Cefalù in Sicily, and in Pisa. The dates cannot be assigned with certainty: the history of art records many a lag, and some architects and masons may have continued to build Romanesque churches while the ogival style was in full career elsewhere. Gothic builders often added a Gothic section to a Romanesque edifice. There was no unity in the Middle Ages even to a country like France, and still less in lands like Italy and Germany, which long remained devoted to their provincialism. True, builders and decorators traveled far and wide, but diversity remained the rule in a divided Europe. Few illusions are more unfounded than the one which, because of the prestige of labels and the convenience of textbooks, leads us to imagine that abbots and masons built in the Romanesque manner, or manners, until a certain date—such as 1200 or 1225—and then suddenly shifted to a new style because a new technique had been devised.

The history of art, like all cultural history, shows a coexistence of three elements acting with varied potency upon the present. The first of these forces is the legacy of the past, with the prestige or traditions, the laggardness of routine, the survival of outworn creeds or rules which can both help and hamper creation. The second is the spread of examples from other regions, even from across the mountains or the seas (in the case of Romanesque art, it may have been Byzantium, Syria, even Iran) mysteriously filtered through to some focal point: Auvergne, or Périgueux, or Toulouse, or Cluny.

But there are also adventurous minds, imaginative spirits who look for new paths and who bring the forces of experiment to bear upon the weight of tradition. They make up the third force. They usually do not emerge isolated in cultural history; the same discovery in science, engineering, philosophical speculation, painting technique, or architecture is effected almost at the same time in parts of the world which seem to be, and are, remote from one another. The first use of the vault in Romanesque art, the first sculptured porches telling the story of the Prophets and of the Apostles, the appearance of the ogival vaults for the first time at Durham, England, or in Normandy, or in Italy around the year 1100—these were not clear-cut events comparable to the accession of a sovereign to a throne or the winning of a decisive battle. They occurred simultaneously at diverse places in Christendom. They were preceded by slow, unseen trial and error. Claims to priority in these matters are often vain, and asserted with not a little childishness. The notion of polygenesis, the more or less simultaneous birth of multiple and similar children of man's genius, is the best key to the understanding of our cultural past.

We may, for clarity's sake, assign the beginnings of Romanesque architecture to the climacteric year 1000 or thereabout and assume that, while the first ogive did appear early in the twelfth century, it was not generally adopted until the end of that century. It took time for the ogive to pass from the reinforced vaults to other parts of the structure, from Norman or Anglo-Norman churches to the edifices built in southern regions which were closer to Roman memories and legacies. Nevertheless, the speed with which Romanesque architecture and sculpture evolved, within fewer than sixty or seventy years, may well astonish us. So can the enormous number of buildings erected: according to some accounts, eighty cathedrals and five hundred churches of considerable size between 1170 and 1270. Within the span of three centuries, from the middle of the eleventh to the middle of the fourteenth, France extracted millions of tons of stone from her soil, erected over a thousand smaller churches and almost as many large ones. A scholar, Jean Gimpel, in "The Cathedral Builders" calculates that a skyscraper of fourteen stories could easily be contained in the unfinished Beauvais cathedral, and that it would take a skyscraper of forty stories to rise up to the top of the Strasbourg spire. The technical achievement, even when full allowance is made for the extraordinary religious inspiration which prompted it, is staggering to the imagination. "No other age ever erected so many and such vast buildings," says Henri Focillon in his remarkable synthesis, "Art of the West."

Our information is relatively scant on who built and inspired or directed the buildings, from what materials and on what funds. But the work was not altogether anonymous. Several "masters of the work" and sculptors like Gislebert at Autun, placed their sign on a relief or on a slab of stone: at times they gave their full names, at other times they drew a sign, a mark which designated a certain team. From such signatures at Bourges, Périgueux, Chauvigny, St. Benoit-sur-Loire, we can follow the wanderings of some artists. We learn that a sizable proportion of them belonged to the Church: Cluny and many a Cistercian monastery sent off abbots and brothers who were professional architects. Suger of St. Denis is the most famous of them. But others were laymen at the service of religious communities or of dukes and counts who decided to erect a shrine. The meager sums which they received have in several cases been recorded in archives.

They did not use elaborate blueprints. Their fancies or their creative impulses were allowed considerable leeway. But coordination was clearly effected at some level. The romantic notion of the people collectively cutting and placing stones and raising a structure as an inspired folk creation is no longer tenable. Some Romanesque reliefs and a painting on the vault of St. Savin have left us picturesque images of a team of masons at work on an actual building or on the Tower of Babel. Wisely interpreted, they are informing as well as entertaining. The expense of making cathedrals higher, bolder and frailer than any in nearby cities eventually proved too much for some communities. Beauvais and Siena were perhaps permanently impoverished by their excessive ambitions. But that was the case only with the Gothic churches, which were financed and erected by the communes in many cases, or by what corresponded to our city councils or municipalities.

In the earlier era of Romanesque shrines, the funds were provided by religious orders, some of which had accumulated immense wealth. That wealth accrued in part from donors and in part from humble pilgrims. At the source of much of the finest medieval art lay the worship of relics: bones of saints, often unearthed from their graves and distributed among several communities which erected churches to house them; objects supposed to have come into contact with the saint: veils of St. Veronica, garments supposed to have been touched by St. Mary Magdalen, pieces of the Cross, etc. It was in order to enable the crowds of worshipers to walk around the choir where relics were housed that space was provided at the eastern end of churches, behind the transept and the altar: the name of this section of a building, the ambulatory, indicated its use. Masterpieces of richly ornamented cabinet-making were wrought and bejeweled to serve as worthy containers for relics. Vézelay owes its existence to the relics of Mary Magdalen, Cologne to those of the Magi, the Sainte-Chapelle to the purchase of the alleged Crown of Thorns in Constantinople by St. Louis, King of France.

The sale and exhibition of these relics entailed many abuses. The credulity of the faithful, plodding their way on pilgrimages toward sanctuaries located thousands of miles away, the squalor of some of their exhausting forced marches, not often relieved by tellers of tales as diverting as those told by Chaucer's travelers, the sacrifices they were asked (and were eager) to make for the sake of their faith or to obtain a miraculous cure, may well arouse either pity or contempt in some of us today. Erasmus, Montaigne, Voltaire and Hume have taught us that disbelief can be healthy, that it can seat faith, after it has victoriously survived scrutiny, more firmly. The men of Conques, Canterbury, Santiago de Compostela and Assisi believed that God, the Virgin, Christ and innumerable saints intervened incessantly in the affairs of this our life. Miracle, in Goethe's oft-quoted phrase in "Faust," was the dearest and natural offspring of faith, *des Glaubens liebstest Kind*.

These observations detract nothing from the extraordinary achievements of Romanesque builders and sculptors, or from their great originality. For superstitions have existed elsewhere; they are probably inseparable from religion when it is cut down to the size of ignorant practitioners; they cannot be, in true justice—which is to say in true charity—taken away from suffering men and women or from individuals in mortal peril. But very few religions, very few ages have witnessed a flowering of art as did the twelfth century in Western Europe. No skeptical irony, no economic view of history can explain it. The United States after the Civil War, France after World War I, Italy after the Risorgimento—all erected thousands of monuments to their dead or to their past. Statues stand in hundreds of European boulevards and parks to commemorate military and other national glories. But little great, or even tolerable, art can be found among these monuments, which were often unstintingly financed. Few eras were favored with such talent and genius inspired by faith as was that which followed the year 1000. Thus art literally preserved for us the image of an era which we, most inadequately, call the Middle Ages.

THE CHURCH OF ST. MAGDALEN

VÉZELAY

Sculpture had been both a forgotten craft and a neglected art during the centuries which elapsed between the end of Greco-Roman antiquity and the Romanesque Renaissance of the eleventh and twelfth centuries. The prohibition of three-dimensional representations of God, of Christ or of man cannot alone account for the dearth of sculpture, for during that period mature craftmanship was displayed in mosaics and paintings.

The Church soon realized how impossible it was, in the lands where pagan traditions had been deeply implanted, to curb the instinctive desire of the believers for representations of their local saints. St. Foy, for example, who was worshipped at her celebrated shrine at Conques in central France, on one of the main roads of pilgrimages, was credited with avenging herself, exacting even the penalty of death, upon the highbrow clerks who attempted to keep the people from paying tribute to her image.

Monumental sculpture reappeared at last in Christian lands early in the twelfth century. That sculpture, along with the ogive vault and the stained glass window, ranks among the most original creations of the Middle Ages in the artistic realm. Its development was rapid and highly varied. It ranged farther than even Hellenic carving had and it was richer in masterpieces than any other flowering of the same art.

As in Renaissance Italy, the first sculptors may have been men trained in the workshops of goldsmiths. We have discovered in the last fifty years tasteful and finely wrought, if somewhat stylized, jewelry made by the Scythians and Sarmatians who lived in the remote steppes of the Urals and in Southern Russia. Their depictions of animals may have penetrated to Western Europe and there inspired the carving of the decoration of Romanesque capitals. The complex, interlaced motifs found in the Celtic miniatures of Ireland, another inheritance from a pre-Christian culture, also may have stimulated the decorative inventiveness of Romanesque sculptors. But the achievement of the men of Vézelay, Autun, Poitiers remains unparalleled, and hardly can be ascribed to any interplay of influences. It stands on its own, brilliantly.

Its chief originality can be seen in the sculptures carved on the porches of cathedrals and on the capitals. These porch sculptures, like Greek caryatids, are integral with the pillars themselves, or are at one with the stone entrance which they adorn and interpret. In many Romanesque churches, the Savior in His majesty or judging the living and the dead arisen on the Last Day is the powerful theme chiseled at the very entrance of the sanctuary: "*Per me transite. Non est via altera vitae.* Pass through here. There is no other way to life." In the majority of churches erected in the twelfth century, the finest sculpture is situated at the portals; inside the edifices, it is

CHRIST IN HIS GLORY. This great sculpture is found on the famous portal which leads from the narthex to the main nave of the basilica of St. Magdalen at Vézelay. It shows the Savior bestowing the Holy Ghost on His apostles so that they may convert the peoples of the earth. The apostles are depicted in a series of compartments around the spandrel and the lintel. Sculpture was frequently done on porches or entrances, where it would be close to the people coming to worship.

ST. MAGDALEN AT NIGHT. The basilica is shown here illuminated in the darkened town of Vézelay. Drawn by the presence of relics of the forgiven sinner St. Mary Magdalen, pilgrims flocked to Vézelay from the church's earliest days. Often they made this a pious stop on a longer pilgrimage to Santiago of Compostella, in northwestern Spain. The present structure is a restoration undertaken in the nineteenth century long after it had been allowed to fall into disrepair.

"THE MYSTICAL MILL." This sculpture at St. Magdalen shows a prophet pouring out the grain of "Old Law" (of the Old Testament) and St. Paul collecting the flour of the New Law.

displayed around the upper part of capitals. It was thus more accessible to the faithful than the much higher sculptures on the pediment of a Greek temple ever were.

Sculpture and architecture, an imposing natural location and a treasure of historical memories combine to make Vézelay one of the hallowed places of France, her Monte Cassino or her Assisi. Lovers of art and the religious youth of France to this day repair to that sacred plateau on pilgrimages.

The abbey at Vézelay, originally Benedictine, was officially consecrated by the Pope in 878. Later it was taken over by the monks of Cluny, the great order of southern Burgundy whose power and prestige were unequaled in the Middle Ages. Vézelay never displayed the luxurious overaffluence for which Cluniac abbeys later came to be notorious. The Cistercians, whose order also originated in Burgundy, fought the ostentatiousness of Cluny. St. Bernard was the Cistercians' greatest representative and his memory is associated with Vézelay.

The importance of Vézelay was based on a history of miracles said to have taken place at the grave where lay the relics of St. Magdalen, the forgiven sinner. Her festival on July 22 was the occasion for a huge celebration. Pilgrims flocked there. There, on March 31, 1146, St. Bernard preached with vibrant eloquence the Second Crusade, in the presence of King Louis VII of France and his nobles. There in 1190, King Philip Augustus of

86

"LEWDNESS AND DESPAIR." A serpent biting a woman represents the punishment awaiting those who are lewd. At the right, the figure of worldly despair pierces his own breast.

France and Richard the Lion Hearted met before departing for the Third Crusade. Earlier, Thomas-à-Becket had solemnly excommunicated Henry II from the Vézelay pulpit. It was at Vézelay that envoys of St. Francis of Assisi founded the first Franciscan convent in France. When other relics of St. Magdalen were announced to have been located in Provence, the abbey lost some of its attraction and affluence. Eventually it fell into abandon. Between 1840 and 1859, it was restored by Viollet-le-Duc, then a young architect of singular audacity.

St. Magdalen offers one of the most imposing views in the whole of France, with the tremendous vistas of the valley of the Cure river and of the Morvan mountains beyond it, the elegant St. Michael tower on the south side, a triple portal, a small cloister and a faultless apse. The porch is one of the most renowned in all the world. Inside, the narthex opens up on the basilica through three portals. The view of the nave and of the choir from there cannot fail but plunge the visitor into a state of exalted wonder.

The central portal has a tympanum which is one of the greatnesses of Vézelay: Christ in His Glory, enormously tall, bestows the Holy Ghost upon the twelve Apostles in the form of rays which radiate from His hands. The eight scenes surrounding the tympanum depict the miracles performed by the Apostles. In the medallions are shown the signs of the zodiac and the tasks done by country people during the different months of the year.

ST. MAGDALEN'S GREAT NAVE. The nave of the basilica is Romanesque; the choir, done later, is Gothic. The two styles are skillfully blended but even so the contrast is striking. The nave is exceptionally long—nearly four hundred feet—and divided into ten bays with groined arches. The bays are separated by semicircular archbands which are made of alternating bright and darker stone.

The peoples of the earth who are to be evangelized have been amusingly portrayed by the fanciful sculptor: some are dwarfs, others half monstrous or otherwise strange. The whole scene breathes dignity and severity, with a fine harmony in the composition. And above all, it is intensely dramatic.

The nave of the basilica, an unusually long one, had to be rebuilt after a fire. This was done in 1120-1140. As a result it is in part Romanesque, and part Gothic in the choir, yet the effect is harmonious. The colors of the stone alternate between a gay lightness and a more severe dark. The contrast between the noble severity of the nave and choir, with slender pillars and brighter lighting, has been ingeniously softened by an architect who, while working in the Gothic manner, pursued the same general effect as his Romanesque predecessor.

The anonymous artists (there may have been as many as five of them) who carved the much admired sculpture on the Vézelay capitals rank among the finest sculptors of the Middle Ages. In addition to the scenes reproduced here, there are sculpted groups showing the building of Noah's Ark, the wicked rich man and Lazarus, Jacob wrestling with the angel, Adam and Eve, and others. A whole bestiary can be descried on those carved stones, and a whole demonology as well, for at times the artists strove to inspire the faithful with fright. At other moments, their aim seems to have been realistic and even gently ironical; they drew their subjects from the familiar agrarian life they saw around them.

There are imperfections in the basilica. Some are due to the wear of time, cruelly aided by the ferocious destructions of the Protestants during the religious wars, and the aftermath of the Revolution which turned the French against a whole phase of their past. Others were created by a well meant but uninspired restoration which copied the appearance of the sculptures of the tympanum but missed the spirit which had animated the artists of old. Even in its original state, the basilica did not make a complete and harmonious whole: the north tower was never finished beyond the first level; the choir was a thirteenth-century addition while the nave was from the early twelfth and the narthex from the middle twelfth. The flying buttresses on the south side are nineteenth-century reconstructions. But it is a characteristic of vigorous, self-confident art to accept its own faults and even to gain from them. The supreme achievement of the men who built that 394-foot-long nave and sculpted those capitals was to express their philosophy and their religion, their sensibility and their dreams—all in one unifying synthesis. And so the image of Christ on the central tympanum, while splendidly concrete and alive, also represents the principle of all creation, the only Unity in a world of change and of struggle.

THE CATHEDRAL OF ST. LAZARUS

AUTUN

The city of Autun in Burgundy lies almost halfway between the Loire and the Saône rivers, between Nevers and Beaune. It entered history as the metropolis of the Gauls, whose last defender, Vercingetorix, surrendered in 52 B.C. to Julius Caesar at Alesia. Under the Romans it soon grew into a prosperous city.

Christianity spread to Burgundy in the fourth century. The Burgundians, invaders who had originally come from the shores of the Baltic Sea, and the Franks became adherents of the new faith. In the eleventh century, a brilliant culture flourished in the province, and it was in the middle of that century the splendid churches of Tournus and Vézelay were erected. Count Girard de Roussillon, the feudal lord who brought the relics of St. Mary Magdalen at Vézelay, brought from Marseilles to Autun the relics of Lazarus, brother of Martha and of Mary.

Another Lazarus is also associated with the cathedral at Autun. He was the poor man in Jesus' parable of the rich man and the poor man. During the Middle Ages this Lazarus came to be thought of as the patron saint of the lepers, and his name is commemorated in the word "lazaretto," a hospital for infectious diseases.

The church of St. Lazarus—or St. Ladre, as he was often called in the Middle Ages—was built between 1120 and 1140 as a shrine for the relics De Roussillon had brought. In 1147, the relics were transferred to the new building in the presence of a crowd so impatient to see them that swords, sticks and fisticuffs were lavishly resorted to; such was, and long remained, the eagerness of the faithful and of pilgrims to draw near these sacred remains. The number of lepers who wanted to crowd into the church of Lazarus was so great, and their presence inside was so feared, that a shelter exposed to the winds, and thus aired, was established for them at the entrance. The sick could thus worship without having to be allowed into the church itself.

The most conspicuous features of St. Lazarus are its storied sculptures on the portal and on the capitals. When they were done cannot be ascertained precisely. The great artist who was the author of most of the Autun sculptures had probably been trained at the abbey of Cluny. He could not well have remained uninformed of or unmoved by what was being achieved at nearby Vézelay when, after a huge fire, the new basilica of St. Mary Magdalen was started there in 1120. As a church, St. Lazarus cannot compare with the stately and pure grandeur of Vézelay; the sculpture, however, is superior in unity of conception and in suppleness of execution. Other Romanesque porches may come close to Autun; none can be pronounced superior to it.

The exterior of St. Lazarus may disappoint those who expect a pure Romanesque building. It underwent a number of alterations. First, buttresses were added when they proved indispensable to strengthen the walls.

Then, in the fifteenth century, the spire collapsed after it had been struck by lightning. (If Benjamin Franklin's invention could have occurred five hundred years earlier, when the only defense against fire was to place the relics of a saint at the top of towers, many of the tallest medieval churches might have been preserved.) A new spire, wholly empty inside so as not to need any woodwork and thus be less of a fire hazard, was erected. The cathedral thus acquired a flamboyant feature. Again in the fifteenth century, part of the choir and the chapels of the right aisle were redone. The two towers of the main portal are a nineteenth-century addition.

The worst architectural havoc was perpetrated at St. Lazarus not by the French Revolution, which lacked the time to demolish it, but by the canons of the church themselves. In the eighteenth century they had no appreciation of medieval art. They were ashamed of Romanesque and Gothic sculptures, which struck them as barbaric. Inside the cathedral at Autun they erected chapels and statues; but the original sculptures they preferred to hide. In 1766, they covered the splendid sculptures of the tympanum with plaster and the apse with marble. Thus they unwittingly helped save what they wished to eradicate.

In 1837, a priest of Autun who was interested in archaeology discovered under the coat of plaster at the entrance portal the Last Judgment. Viollet-le-Duc undertook a restoration that began in 1858. He carried out his task with discretion and praiseworthy fidelity to what remained of the original. In 1939, the marble coatings which marred the Romanesque apse were lifted. Later still, in 1948, the head of the figure of Christ on the portal, which had been summarily cut off by the canons of the chapter in the eighteenth century, was recovered from the Rolin museum in Autun and placed back where it belonged.

Much research has been done since then on Autun and on the genius who sculpted the tympanum and most of the capitals inside. It happens that the name of that artist is known to us: he carved on the portal the words *Gislebertus hoc fecit* ("This is the work of Gislebertus"). His name has been rendered into French as Gislebert or Gillebert. We know nothing of his life or career, except that he stands as one of the true geniuses in the whole range of the history of art. André Malraux has said of him: "Gislebert is not a primitive—but a Romanesque Cézanne." His art, indeed, bears no traces of awkwardness; there is no unevenness among the different subjects which he treated with a calm felicity akin to that of a Mozart or of a Bach. Most of his work must have been completed within some ten years, and by an artist at the peak of powers, for it is impossible to perceive any evolution in his creations. While other medieval artists signed their work, wishing to be remembered

AT JUDAS' SIDE. Pictured in stone in a crouch at the body of
Judas, who has just hanged himself in despair, is a grimacing devil.
This is considered one of the masterpieces of Romanesque sculpture.

by posterity, the proud assertion of authorship by Gislebert and the strong marks of one personality in the
planning and execution of the varied sculptures of St. Lazarus—sacred and profane, grave and humorous—constitute a unique case in the history of art. Vézelay, Moissac, St. Sernin at Toulouse were all the result of
collective creation. The inventiveness and the originality of Gislebert remain unexplained.

    While the celebrated porch at Vézelay portrays Christ endowing His apostles with the Holy Spirit and
sending them to evangelize the earth, thus symbolizing the dawn of the new Christian world, the tympanum of
Gislebert at Autun depicts with austere force the end of the world and the Judgment at which rewards and punishments will be meted out. But there is little bustle and chaos in his rendering of what the poet John Donne, in
"The Relique," calls "the last busie day." The tympanum is made up of twenty-nine precisely fitted stones;
their enormous weight made it necessary to set up a post, or "trumeau," in the middle to support the lintel.

    The main theme is the Judgment, being pronounced by a very tall Christ, His arms outstretched. Three
Latin inscriptions of two lines each make the meaning clear: Christ is the sole judge; some who have not led an
impious life will be reborn to an eternal life; the others should be filled with dread at seeing here the torments
which await them. The Virgin is seated on the right of Christ; on His left are two figures, perhaps those of Elias
and Enoch, said to have been taken alive to Heaven.

    Above them to the right and left are angels, the traditional messengers of the Day of Doom, blowing their
long trumpets. Another angel wields his sword to reject the damned and preserve the band of the elect against
intrusion. The dead arise, most of them naked. Some bear the familiar insignia of pilgrims: the Cross and the
shell of St. James. Children implore an angel to let them in. A wife holds her husband's hand, and touchingly
points to their child, feebly emerging from the slumber of death.

    In the group of the damned, fear and remorse are powerfully rendered. This section has the greatest
impact upon visitors to St. Lazarus. Fear, perhaps the most potent of all emotions, but seldom expressed in sculpture, is imparted to the onlooker as he stands here. He sees faces that are aghast, with haggard eyes, such as that
of the wretched mortal awakening from his grave only to have his throat gripped by the two monstrous hands of
a demon. A miser, his bag of gold around his neck, writhes in a serpent's coil. A lustful woman has her breasts
bitten by snakes. The Devil, repulsive, only partly human in shape, with the triple head of a viper, seizes a dead
man by his hair. The weighing of the souls was a traditional theme in sculptures of the Judgment and none has

THE FALL OF THE SORCERER. Gislebert's working of this famous legend shows what happened to Simon the Magician in his search for marvelous powers *(opposite page)*. After St. Peter spurned Simon's bribes the Devil gave him wings. But St. Peter *(shown at the left with his key)* and St. Paul prayed that the power of flight be withdrawn. Simon comes plunging down, where a horned fiend waits him.

THE DAMNED. Still arising with difficulty from the sleep of death, the doomed souls, all of them unclad, many clutching their heads, *(below)* start for Hell after the Last Judgment. Hurrying the rejected ones along on their journey is an angel with wings outstretched and brandishing a sword. This sculpture is a section from the awesome tympanum at Autun which depicts the end of the world and the ultimate destiny of souls.

ON THE DAY OF WRATH. The horrors of Judgment Day are vividly seen in the Autun sculpture. The carving on the opposite page shows a wretch emerging from his grave to be gripped by the monstrous hands of a demon. The condemned man's eyes bulge, his mouth twists in a scream.

EVE THE TEMPTRESS. The painted relief of a sensuous Eve is half of what was the lintel of the north portal of St. Lazarus. The other half, now lost, portrayed Adam, listening to her seductive whispers as she prepares to take the apple. The work is now in the Rolin museum at Autun. (Pages 100-101)

been rendered with more imaginative intensity than Gislebert's. The demons slyly try to apply their weight on the scale so as to steal a worthy soul from St. Michael. Another demon holds an adulterous woman, also bitten by a snake, at the tip of his fork. From a demon's caldron arms and legs protrude. There is seldom any pity expressed in medieval art for the endless torments of the damned in hell. The artists sought to frighten would-be adulterous wives with the assurance that relentless punishments would follow wicked or wayward lives.

The bestiary of St. Lazarus at Autun, like that of Vézelay, is rich and also original, since ancient artists had seldom represented any other animal than the horse. The bestiary's significance is symbolic; but it is also, and more, an expression of man's affinity with his lower brothers. All barriers between the real and the fantastic are obliterated. Unicorns, phoenixes, and dragons as well as demons and other ministers of Satan populated the imagination of Gislebert and his contemporaries. The porch and the capitals at St. Lazarus display one of the weirdest examples of the "art of the visionaries," as they were termed by the great historian and interpreter of Romanesque and Gothic art, Henri Focillon.

Visionaries like Gislebert, or Michelangelo or El Greco or, much later, Van Gogh and Odilon Redon, effortlessly distort the size and the proportions of the objects and persons which their art endows with a new life. It would be naïve to wonder why the sculptor of St. Lazarus represented Christ, as Milton does Satan in "Paradise Lost," "above the rest proudly eminent" and altered the proportions which any likeness to reality or to our usual idea of the divine would suggest as reasonable. The space available on a tympanum, like the space of the triangular pediment of a Greek temple, required both curtailment and magnification. Strong contrasts and differences in emphasis had to be provided. The sculptor of Autun was attempting to convey, through unmistakable and visible forms, the spiritual superiority of the Son of Man over ordinary mortals. His sculpture is powerfully dramatic without being declamatory. It reveals a superb technical mastery, but the technique remains subservient to the imaginative translation of his vision of the world where good, rewarded by the Redeemer, was to triumph over evil.

A vast diversity of scenes are chiseled on the archivolts and on the capitals of St. Lazarus. The signs of the zodiac, representations of the seasons, and intricate decorative foliage appear on the medallions. It seems that these sculptures were not, as at Vézelay, done on the medallions when they were already placed, but on stones which were subsequently lifted to their present positions. This added to the difficulties of the sculptor, who had to envision in his mind his completed work from the angle at which it would be seen when in position.

Several of the capitals at Autun must be rated as jewels of Romanesque sculpture. One on the southern wall portrays the hanging of Judas. It corresponds to God questioning Cain on another capital and embodies the same lesson: the punishment of an atrocious crime. The naked body of the traitor hangs lamentably from a tree, his head bent, his mouth gaping. Two hideous demons, grinning, pull a rope tied to the round purse containing the thirty silver coins received by Judas as the price for his betrayal. Volutes of flowers on each side, above the winged demons with their bulging, enormous heads, add an ironically idyllic touch to the gruesome scene. The original of this sculpture of Judas, along with some other originals, is kept in a room above the vestry at Autun. Faithful copies were put in their place in the church in the nineteenth century, when it proved necessary to erect new pillars in order to strengthen the structure.

One incident related in the Acts of the Apostles that often served as a picturesque theme for medieval carvers concerns Simon Magus, a magician who, once christened, attempted to bribe St. Peter to provide him with supernatural powers. He was rebuked by St. Peter. A later legend added that Simon Magus secured assistance from the Devil and flew off into the air. Peter and Paul then prayed to have his magical power withdrawn from him. Nowhere is this story more vividly presented than on two capitals at Autun. On one the two saints, with St. Peter holding his key, look up to heaven while the would-be thaumaturgist ascends on double wings. The end of the story shows Simon tumbling down, head first, from his rash ascent, as the saints watch gleefully. He is awaited by a horned devil, squatting and grinning. This capital was meant as a tribute to the wisdom and power of the two saints as well as a warning to the many practitioners of sorcery in the Middle Ages.

Three examples of sculpture on the pillars of Autun are free from snakes, monsters and demons. They are renowned for the loveliness of the scenes depicted with touching details, and for the naïve simplicity of an art which stands close to popular inspiration. They show how deeply the imagination of common men and women was impressed, in those far-off centuries, by the human anecdotes from the life of Christ. The three subjects are drawn from the Gospel of St. Matthew. They relate to the birth and childhood of Jesus. The Adoration of the Magi in the church is a copy of the original which is now in the room above the vestry; so is the most famous of all the capitals of St. Lazarus, the Flight into Egypt. The Sleep of the Magi in the church is original.

The Adoration shows the Magi offering their presents to the newborn baby. One of them, old and grave in appearance, kneels; his arms and hands, beautifully modeled, present his gift of perfume in a large round vase. The second king, much younger and with a look of wonder on his face, touches his crown with his left hand as a gesture of salute to the miraculous birth and offers a smaller vase than the first. The third of the wise men of the East, bearded, a gleam of serene joy in his eyes, steps forward with a vivid gesture. He holds what could be a big rectangular book, or, more probably, a small casket.

It has been argued by some art historians that his present might be the book handed by God to the first man, promising his eventual deliverance. But symbolic and extreme interpretations of this sort concerning medieval art are usually less tenable than the obvious and perfectly adequate ones. The presents reported by St. Matthew are myrrh, incense and gold. The small, rectangular casket contains the most precious gift which the unsophisticated king could offer: gold. The sculpture shows Mary holding on her lap the Infant Jesus. His little feet emerge from the swaddling clothes. With eager eyes He watches the king bowing before Him and He places His tiny hand on the vase. Behind these figures sits Joseph with his head resting on his right arm which in turn rests on his knee. Joseph, wearing a cap such as a medieval artisan might wear, observes the scene wide-eyed, obviously puzzled.

The three kings, Matthew relates, were warned in a dream not to return to Herod who had earlier directed them to Bethlehem. They went home by another route. The angel sent to warn them is shown on another capital, pointing to the star which would guide the travelers on their return. The three kings lie close to each other, their heads touching, with their crowns on their heads so as to be clearly identifiable. They have gone to sleep under one blanket. The bed, its wooden posts, its canopy, the folds of the blanket are sculpted with striking realism. But the fidelity to everyday details, which gives the scene a rustic charm, only serves to bring out the essentials: the inspired expression of the angel and the thoughtful, grave faces of the three kings who have been favored with a divine warning. Two are still asleep, with heavy eyelids and calm features. The youngest one, on the left, is awake, and stares as he hears the warning of the angel. (This capital, incidentally, still bears a few faint traces of color. Like the others, it must have been polychromous in its original condition.)

For the scene of the Flight into Egypt the story is again drawn from the second chapter of the first Gospel. Joseph walks ahead, his carpenter's tools on his shoulder; he looks weary, emaciated. In his right hand, he holds a rope by which he leads the donkey. The animal is wonderfully expressive, full of mettle, proud of the burden which it is carrying. On the donkey rides Mary, her head leaning to one side and surrounded with a halo. Her cheeks are full, her eyes are rapt in a dream. She holds the Baby with her left arm on her lap. With

THE ADORATION OF THE MAGI. The sculptures
which relate the childhood of Jesus in St. Lazarus' Cathedral
are done in an amiable, lighthearted spirit which probably
reflects the attitude of the people of the time to the Gospels.
The reverence of the kings is clear as they present their gifts
of myrrh, incense and gold. But there is a beguiling touch in
the king in the background who tips his crown to the Child.

THE WARNING TO THE MAGI. After the adoration the kings retired and, still wearing their crowns, put their heads on a single pillow and slept under a single blanket. In their dreams they were visited by an angel who warned them not to return to Herod's palace but to take another route in going home. Now, while two of the kings still sleep, the third is awake with the excitement of the news.

THE FLIGHT. Mary and Jesus, looking serious and pensive on their flight into Egypt, ride a spirited, mettlesome donkey, obviously proud of the sacred burden it is carrying. It is part of the charm of this sculpture, one of the reasons why it has become one of the most popular works in medieval Christian art, that the donkey seems to be moving along without moving its legs, much like the little wooden wheeled donkeys that are part of everyone's childhood.

His tiny right hand, Jesus, who is sculpted full-faced, with eyes already deeply serious, lightly touches the symbolic globe held by His mother. A strip of flowers and fruits fills the left side of the picture. Circular, wheel-shaped supports, five in number, are seen in the lower part of the sculpture. They may be a purely decorative motif or, as some scholars have surmised, a recollection by the artist of the small chariots on which Christ was shown being drawn by a donkey in some French villages on Palm Sunday.

Near St. Lazarus is a rich museum in what was once the mansion of Chancellor Nicolas Rolin. This fifteenth-century magistrate is associated with several masterpieces of art: the great polyptych of "The Last Judgment" by Roger van der Weyden in the hospital at Beaune, "The Nativity" by the Master of Moulins in which the Chancellor's son, a bishop of Autun, is pictured as a donor, and a splendid painting by Van Eyck, now in the Louvre, in which the chancellor himself is protrayed near the "Virgin of Autun." The Rolin museum at Autun is now the home of one of the finest nudes sculpted in the Middle Ages. It is Gislebert's Eve. It once was positioned on the north lintel of St. Lazarus as part of a relief representing Adam and Eve. This lintel was taken away from the cathedral and not retrieved until 1866 from a house then being demolished. By then only half of it remained. The loss of half of a splendid sculpture which must have been over eight feet long is one of the most deplorable in the whole range of Burgundian Romanesque art.

As we have the work today, Eve is seen lying on the ground, preparing to pluck an apple from the branch which Satan (not visible in this remnant) has bent to tempt her. She holds her hand close to her mouth, as if to explain something in secret to Adam. This rendering of man's and woman's first disobedience and of the consequent Fall deserves to rank among the most impressive in Christian art. So attractive is the face of Eve, with her flowing hair, her limbs, the realistic modeling of her body with only a vine leaf as a covering, her reclining attitude, that this nude might have been inspired by some sculpture from pagan antiquity. It reveals in Gislebert a master able to chisel sensuous bodies just as superbly as he did episodes from the childhood of Jesus, visionary scenes of men preyed upon by devils, of Satan ready to work his mischief within every one of us, and of the dead arising to be judged. This great man of the Romanesque was the enigmatic predecessor of the many moderns who have pondered the disturbing legend of Lazarus brought back from the world of the departed and holding the secrets of the life beyond the grave. Gislebert did his tremendous work four hundred years before the Elizabethan dramatists of England so anxiously yearned, as John Webster wrote, for "but two days' conversation with the dead."

THE CHURCH OF SAN ZENO

VERONA

Few clichés are so complacently accepted and handed down from one nostalgic yearner for the past to another as that concerning the "unity" of medieval culture. According to this misconception, the men and women of western Europe were then at peace with themselves and with each other; they accepted one faith, one philosophy and they all acclaimed the Romanesque style when they lived in what we retrospectively call the Romanesque era. But history can authoritatively demonstrate that the truth is not so.

Then, as now, creativeness sprang from diversity and from the assertion of individual differences. The builders of Auvergne differed markedly from those of western France and even from those of Provence, where other materials were available and where Roman models and traditions weighed more heavily. Masons and sculptors from Italy in the twelfth century had as many points of variance as they had of similarities with those of Vézelay and Autun. The themes were of course the same all over Christendom; the didactic intention of the ecclesiastical hierarchy was similar in the north and the south. But the intervention of the divine or of saints in human affairs was not everywhere conceived in the same way. And art, which is, in Henri Focillon's phrase, "the life of forms," varied greatly from region to region. Geographical or social conditions do not offer an adequate explanation for such diversity; no force of history accounts for it. We fall back upon a mysterious entity which we call the national temper, itself made up of a great many conflicting forces, and see it reflected in art.

The few data traditionally put forth as an explanation of the variety in Italian Romanesque all have some validity: the country, once unified under Roman administration, law and army, later became far more divided than either England or France. Municipal life thrived with more intensity here than elsewhere in Europe. There were rivalries between Florence and Pisa, Siena and the neighboring Tuscan cities, Verona and Milan. The country as a whole paid a heavy price for political turbulence.

However, it might be said that the Italians, like the French before them, and perhaps the Germans after them, compensated with creativeness for their inability to unite politically despite the constant peril stemming from better organized if more uncouth enemies surrounding them. We marvel to this day over the originality of Verona as compared to Pisa, Modena, or Milan, at the independence of each of the three or four striking churches in Verona itself, and fall to lamenting our own age of conformity, a conformity which includes an obsession with anxiety.

The builders in Italy inevitably encountered ancient traditions everywhere around them. They resorted freely to the inexhaustible quarries of stones, already hewn, which they found in the Roman Colosseum or in the

A JEWEL IN BRONZE AND MARBLE. Verona's Benedictine Church of San Zeno, the patron of Italian cities, dates from the twelfth century. It is rich in sculpture and painting, but the essence of its Romanesque beauty lies in its western doorway. The porch is supported by two thin columns resting on the backs of crouching lions below. The bronze tableaux on the doors and the marble bas-reliefs surrounding them treat of all manner of things from the Old and New Testament, the fall of Adam and Eve, the Descent of Christ from the Cross. There are also knightly combats and incidents from the ancient history of Verona, such as that which is shown on the page opposite. Here the Emperor Galen, in gratitude to St. Zeno for driving a devil out of his daughter, offers his imperial crown to the saint.

Verona amphitheatre. They could not help studying the Pantheon, the Baths of Caracalla and other monuments surviving from Roman times. Nor could they easily avoid the impact of pagan mythology, concretely tangible in statues and reliefs dug up from their soil. The people themselves and their priests would not and could not separate Christian saints from ancient local heroes who had been deified.

This survival of antiquity was nowhere else in Europe experienced to the same extent, and to it we must probably ascribe the close participation of the Italian people in their local art. The closeness of this participation was unmatched beyond the Alps, even at the time of the Crusades. André Chastel, one of the most penetrating interpreters of Italian art in recent times, has stressed the secular character of many a representation of the Virgin as a frightened girl heeding the Annunciation of a messenger; the Madonna is like almost any Italian mother with her infant, the women weeping over Christ's death could be at an ordinary funeral. This realism instilled life and naturalness into the art of the peninsula, in contrast to the stylization of Byzantium or the gravity of Spain.

The churches of Italy, with their façades hardly incorporated into the buildings themselves, look pleasingly outward, to the public square in front, the arcades, the campanile or the baptistery where people stroll or attend to their daily pursuits. These churches have little of the majesty of Moissac, Saint-Gilles or Tournus. Cistercian exhortations for purity and severity in architecture never achieved enduring results in Italy. The faithful insisted upon the multiplication of chapels for their proliferating saints. They demanded rich, colorful ceilings, frescoes and paintings in the different chapels. And they wanted mosaics. Sculpture and painting were thus more closely associated here with architecture than elsewhere.

When the Gothic tide spread to Italy, it produced appealing examples of original buildings in what may be called half-hearted, or Italian, Gothic. But the essential traits of the Gothic of France, England or Germany were soon altered, and the Italian architects returned to the basilica type of structure, with a façade directed at the square outside and a broad nave, but with few ogival vaults or buttresses.

Among the five or six great Romanesque churches in northern Italy, San Zeno at Verona occupies an eminent place. To many moderns, Verona conjures up visions of "Romeo and Juliet": obstinate lovers defying the prohibitions of hostile families, voluptuous strains of nightingales on a summer evening. "The very balconies there seem to be awaiting silken ladders," wrote Théophile Gautier. We do not know whether the two families, fierce partisans of the Pope or of the emperor, Guelphs and Ghibellines, even existed early in the fourteenth

BALAAM'S ASS. The sculpture at San Zeno offers the passers-by homilies from the Bible. In the one shown on this page, Balaam's ass, the embodiment of patience and resignation, the symbol of all those who bear their human troubles philosophically, stares in astonishment. The ass has just heard the angry Balaam curse Israel. And soon the ass will rebuke Balaam.

century. Dante, who then lived in Verona as an exile, apparently knew nothing of them. But the city had much earlier owed some fame to another poet, Catullus, the first in Europe who sang the contradictions of hate and love. Verona had just become a Roman colony, in 89 B.C., when he wrote.

Verona's location just south of the Alps, whose snowy tops are visible from its bridges, has long made it the gateway to the peninsula and to "the land where lemon trees bloom" for the visitors from the Germanic world to the north. Standing as it did in the path of the barbarians, Verona suffered from their exactions after the fall of Rome. However, the city always enjoyed the good fortune of being liked and favored by its conquerors: by Constantine, who defeated Maxentius nearby in 312; by Theodoric, who defeated Odoacer in 489 and developed such a fancy for the city that he preferred it to his capital, Ravenna; by Charlemagne, who established his son Pepin there as a ruler of Italy. Bonaparte was another conqueror who fell in love with Verona. He passed through it in 1805 on his way to be crowned as King of Italy and ordered the restoration of its famous amphitheatre.

The patron saint of San Zeno was honored by a chapel built over his grave as early as the end of the fourth century. It must have been laid waste when the Lombards overran the city and its original population of Ligurians and Venetians in the fifth century. A new shrine for the relics of the saint was erected under Pepin's rule; the Hungarians, in 900, were the destroyers of this one. The present San Zeno church was begun in the eleventh century, the period during which Verona took part in the Lombard League which was sponsored by the papacy against the Holy Roman Empire and Frederic Barbarossa.

The basilica of San Zeno was raised between the end of the eleventh century and 1138; the wooden roof was completed later; and the apse was altered late in the fourteenth century. But the singular beauty of that Romanesque masterpiece must have been manifest to the proud Veronese by the middle of the twelfth century. The campanile, on the right side of the church, is slim and colorful, with only two rows of three windows at the top of its horizontal painted layers. It has few equals in Italy. The roof inside is not vaulted; the construction here is carpentry work supported both by slender columns and more massive pillars. Votive frescoes, many of which were once half erased but have since been restored, decorate the walls. They appear to have been painted by artists torn between the lasting prestige of Byzantine art and the more dramatic manner of Giotto and his followers. Some of the frescoes of San Zeno date from the fourteenth century. The fresco of the Descent from the Cross is a work of undeniable refinement; but it pales beside the sculpture of Christ being taken down from the Cross.

The façade and the portal provide the chief claim of San Zeno to rank among the great Romanesque shrines. The simplicity of the façade, made of tufa, flanked by two slender columns resting on crouching lions, has great attraction for moderns weary of the over-rich ornamentation of late Gothic and of baroque monuments. On its marble panels, a Last Judgment and a wheel of fortune have been carved. Figures are thrust upward or thrown downward by the capricious movements of fortune's wheel. The miracles performed by San Zeno are represented in the lunettes. Scenes from the Scriptures and elsewhere are sculpted on panels at the doorway.

But the rarest splendor of San Zeno shines in its portal. It is surmised that there must have been several artists who worked on it, at least three. One, coming after the earlier masters, probably altered and completed their work. Research has unearthed next to nothing which might enlighten us on the identity of the artists.

The variety of themes among the forty-eight rectangles chiseled on the two sides of the portal is bewildering. Two are forceful, fierce masks, one of a lion and one of a man, which reveal that the attraction of ugliness had impressed artists long before the grotesques of Gothic cathedrals, Hieronymus Bosch or Goya. Other sculptures portray episodes of the life of San Zeno. The expressions of faces, the gestures, the folds of draperies do not have the rich subtlety of the best carvings at Autun. But despite their rigidity and naïvete, they reveal an artist endowed with the power to render volume and mass and the gift to simplify as well.

On one side of the portal are subjects from the Book of Genesis: the creation of Eve, her temptation, her condemnation with Adam, and the expulsion from Eden. The tree of knowledge and flower motifs decorate the left and the lower part of the scene. The angel in his wrath, disymmetrically presented, occupies the center of the panel. Adam exhibits something awkward, animal-like, in his reluctant steps out of Paradise, as if he could not fully gather the significance of his disobedience. Eve, afflicted, in no way beautified by the artist, starts on her way to suffering and remorse. Elsewhere, Abraham's sacrifice, Cain and Abel, Aaron and Moses are sculpted.

There is more emotion in the scenes inspired by the New Testament. The artist, or artists, here reached a completely satisfying harmony between feeling and technique, between the intensity of the symbolic drama enacted and the familiar naturalness of the details. The luxurious ornamentation of St. Mark's at Venice, the refined and self conscious complexity of Orcagna's or the San Michele tabernacle at Florence, even the celebrated panel of Ghiberti for the second door of the baptistery in the same city, all of a more mature and surer workmanship, cannot eclipse the accomplishment of the anonymous sculptor or sculptors who worked at San Zeno in Verona.

THE CHURCH OF ST. SAVIN

SAINT-SAVIN-SUR-GARTEMPE

It is difficult to say which of the many arts that Frenchmen have practiced with mastery over a thousand years and with a continuity unequaled elsewhere expresses the country and its people most completely. Some students of France would be inclined to select sculpture; others would nominate literature; still others might maintain that France is primarily a land of architects. But there is no question that the artistic product of France best known and most admired abroad is painting.

It was long believed that the French talent for painting emerged late in the history of the country, as music emerged relatively late in Germany. While the earliest Sienese and Florentine masters were producing fine Italian frescoes in the early fourteenth century, French art of that period was considered to have been limited to the creation of miniature illuminations in manuscripts, stained-glass windows and tapestries. Until not very long ago, most histories of French painting ignored the Middle Ages altogether.

In the last hundred years, however, scholars, photographers and art curators have uncovered the existence of a rich flowering of painting which accompanied and in some cases preceded the creation of Romanesque architecture and sculpture in France and in a number of other places throughout Europe. Mosaics and frescoes clothed the walls of churches as early as the Merovingian era, although almost none of these has survived. Carolingian art was even more brilliant, if we can judge from what should be considered impressive evidence: the Utrecht Psalter, the mosaics of Germigny-des-Prés in Orleanais and the paintings lately discovered at Saint-Germain of Auxerre, which have been traced back to the year 855. Paintings of the tenth century are still visible at the Oberzell church on the German island of Reichenau and at the Goldbach chapel near Lake Constance. Others survive at Saint-John of Müstair, also in Switzerland.

It is clear that polychromous decoration was used in Europe in the Middle Ages, just as it had been in Greece during the much admired Classical Age. Even the Cistercians, notoriously hostile to color and to anything like it, on the grounds that it was equivalent to indulging in luxury, permitted manuscripts to be illuminated. The painting of that time was considered strictly functional; it could be "read" by people who could read nothing else. *Pictura est quaedam litteratura illiterato,* observed Walafrid Strabo in the ninth century: "A picture is as literature to the illiterate."

Unfortunately, much of the Romanesque painting has been destroyed by the ravages of time, and even more by the indifference or stupidity of men. The crypt of Tavant long served as a barn for hay; the church of

SAINT SAVIN'S GLORIOUS MURALS. The strong but restrained beauty of St. Savin is admirably attuned to the old bridge and to the reflections of both church and bridge in the Gartempe River. The fame of this church is based mainly on its glorious mural paintings, the largest display of Romanesque frescoes on French soil. Some of them, scenes from the Old Testament, can be seen in the shadowy barrel vault 45 feet above the sunlit floor of the nave. Others cover the walls and ceilings of other parts of the church, the porch, altar platform and crypt. But these wonderful adornments do not put the church itself in the pale: it, too, is splendid.

Vic as a storage vault for wheat; Berzé was a storehouse for wood. The religious wars of the sixteenth century and the wrath of revolutionaries later destroyed a number of paintings in abbeys. Many ecclesiastics of the eighteenth century were simply embarrassed by the frescoes of their churches. They considered them primitive as works of art and had them painted over or destroyed. The nineteenth century author Prosper Mérimée, to whom we owe the discovery and ultimately the preservation of many old French monuments, rightly condemned these destroyers, who did not even have the excuse of being barbarians or warriors. "Neither the iconoclastic fury of the Protestants nor the stupid vandalism of the Revolution has left on our monuments such deplorable traces as has the bad taste of the eighteenth and of the nineteenth centuries," he wrote in 1845. The writings of Mérimée made the French authorities effectively ashamed of the neglect into which early paintings had fallen, and better care has been taken of them since.

The finest ensemble of frescoes left to us from the Middle Ages are to be found at St. Savin, which has been called the Romanesque Sistine Chapel. The systematic study of St. Savin was initiated by two great masters of medieval archeology. One was Emile Mâle, who contributed a chapter on mural paintings to a history of art published in 1905; the other, his successor at the Sorbonne, was Henri Focillon, who published a brilliant illustrated monograph on the same subject in 1938. Following in their footsteps a number of scholars have studied the paintings at St. Savin.

We shall probably never know why some regions of the West were more successful than others in producing painters or in attracting them. Within France, artistic talent emerged most brilliantly in four regions. One was Auvergne; a second was Catalonia; Burgundy was another. But by far the most striking accomplishments of painters, at least in the Romanesque era, seem to have taken place in west-central France around Vic, in the Berry region, at Tavant in Touraine (where the wear and tear of time has not totally obscured the intense, almost mystical expressionism of an artist of genius), and at Le Liget, also in Touraine, where Henry II of England founded an abbey in expiation of the murder of Thomas à Becket.

The dominant note in what must once have been an extremely rich covering of paintings is one of serene and stately beauty and of humane tenderness. None of these churches, however—nor the chapel of St. Gilles near Montoire, of which Ronsard was the abbot, and which has a tragic fresco of Christ in Judgment inspired by the Book of Revelation—equals St. Savin in variety, in forcefulness, in genius. For greatness in religious

THE MIGHTIEST OF BATTLES. On the porch appear scenes from the Apocalypse, among them this swirling fresco, which brings movement to the rushing words of St. John the Divine : "'And there was war in heaven : Michael and his angels fought against the dragon ; and the dragon fought and his angels. And prevailed not ; neither was their place found any more in heaven. And the great dragon was cast out, that old serpent called the Devil and Satan, which deceiveth the whole world : he was cast out into the earth and his angels were cast out with him."

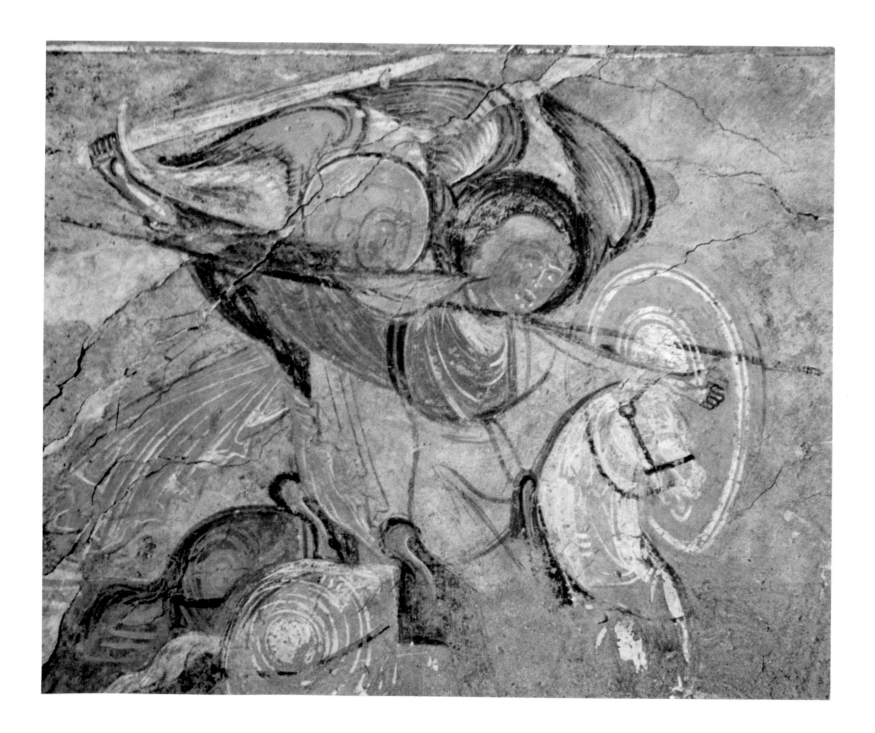

ANGELS IN ADORATION. In the curving tympanum above the door leading from the porch to the interior of the church is a fresco from which the detail shown below was taken. As in the case of St. Michael in battle on the previous page it is remarkable for the graceful and fluid sense of movement it gives to the angels. The three figures are depicted in the act of genuflecting and the graceful curves of their backs just fit the curving surface the artist had to fill. The mural as a whole shows Christ in His Glory in a heavenly Jerusalem with His apostles.

THE WOE OF THE LOCUSTS. The masters of St. Savin found powerful inspiration in the Revelation of St. John. His words and his style ring through the painting reproduced below: "And the shapes of the locusts were like unto horses prepared unto battle; and on their heads were as it were crowns like gold and their faces were as the faces of men. And they had hair as the hair of women and their teeth were as the teeth of lions. And they had breastplates, as it were breastplates of iron; and the sound of their wings was as the sound of chariots. . . ."

THE MOTHER AND THE DRAGON. The painting on the opposite page, like that of the plague of the locusts, is taken from Revelation. It depicts the appearance in the skies of the woman "clothed with the sun, and the moon under her feet and upon her head a crown of twelve stars." A great fiery dragon rushes to devour her newborn infant but she gives it to the angel shown at the left. She herself has already received wings to fly to a hiding place. Some think that the story is symbolical, with the woman representing the Church and the child Christ.

THE GENTLE LIONS. Pictures of the woes foretold in the Apocalypse warned the faithful to lead good lives. Pictures of the gentle lions shown below promised them that in days of trial and tribulation Heaven would not remain deaf to their prayers. They could leave the church renewed in hope and courage. The picture, in the crypt, is one of a series showing the martyrdom of Saints Savin and Cyprian on the banks of the Gartempe River (see pages 134, 135). At one point they are thrown to the lions but the lions come forward and meekly lick their feet.

THE VOYAGE OF NOAH'S ARK. In a ship whose planks are carefully joined and nailed, and which carries a figurehead, Noah and his wife, his sons Shem, Ham and Japheth and their wives, plus a pair of everything, "clean beasts and of beasts that are not clean, and of fowls and of everything that creepeth upon the earth," ride out a 150-day storm. Floating around in the water are the bodies of the drowned. The artist has introduced two giants, perhaps to help Noah, perhaps to help him sink. But the dove is returning with its olive branch; the storm is over.

paintings of what history records as the Romanesque period, one must go to this small community. It has a charm quite apart from its significance in religious art.

The little town of St. Savin, sleepy and placid amid its fields of grain and its pasture lands, is watered by the Gartempe, a narrow and picturesque river which flows into the Creuse. The church stands near the lazy stream and its floating water lilies; the best view of its choir and chevet is from the rustic bridge behind it. St. Savin is a well proportioned and harmonious church, with a long triple nave of nine bays, an ambulatory onto which five chapels open, a transept and a square tower at the cross of the transept. Two curious features attract the visitor's attention. One is the direction of the building: the church does not extend in a straight line to the east where the altar is, but slants slightly southward. The other is the presence of a second tower, very tall and topped by a Gothic spire, which was clearly a later addition. It rises at the entrance of the building, on the west, and constitutes the porch. There were other additions made after the time of the Romanesque. At the end of the eleventh century, the nave was probably prolonged to the tower and the porch was vaulted. There was no tympanum then, but one was subsequently added.

The paintings reproduced here cover the walls of the porch and the center of the tympanum. The porch has been called the Apocalypse of St. Savin. The reason is that the painter derived his themes from Revelation: among his themes on the porch are St. Michael and the dragon, and angels adoring the Lord. On the northern side of the porch, another scene from the Book of Revelation is depicted: the plague of the locusts. An angel clothed in a white robe and a red mantle, with wings unfurled, blows his trumpet in an arresting gesture. He has just lifted the lid of the well of the abyss from which come the locusts, with human faces, lions' teeth and scorpions' tails. The colors are ingeniously contrasted: the well itself is yellow; its lid, shaped like a shield, is brown; the sun is a yellow disc surrounded by white clouds. Two groups of men are pictured, some lying on the ground with their heads turned toward the horrible well, others prostrate on the right. This powerful scene has been compared with the most famous of representations from the Book of Revelation, considered by most experts to be the one shown on the Angers tapestry of the late fourteenth century.

The mother and the dragon is another illustration of a famous verse in Revelation. A dragon with seven heads, ten horns and seven halos threatens the woman. She has just given birth to the Child and holds Him on her lap; He tries to reach the angel with His little hands and the angel seizes them to take Him to God. The

ABRAHAM AND LOT. The Patriarch and his servants have just put to flight the four kings who captured his nephew Lot. Lot is shown on the left pressing forward to embrace his brown-clad uncle, while on the right the defeated forces of the raiding kings gallop away from the battlefield in massed ranks.

130

feet of the woman rest on a crescent moon. In the sky above, a yellow, green and white structure stands for God's sanctuary: the arch of alliance, in the form of a reliquary, is visible inside it. St. John, seated at the left, watches the scene, aghast. The whole fresco is vibrant with life.

Inside the church, the paintings extend along the entire length of the nave, in four rows, two on each side. Some, damaged by centuries of dampness, have almost entirely disappeared. Art lovers will always deplore the loss, for the missing pictures were greatly praised by Mérimée, in whose time they were still fairly clear. They dealt with the creation of the world, showing God, in a vast semicircle strewn with stars, calling into being the sun and the moon, and subsequently presenting Eve to Adam.

Much speculation was once aroused by the fact that both Adam and Eve were apparently painted wearing beards. Some scholars suggested that the beards resulted from a literal approach to the assertion of St. Augustine and other theologians that virtue is recognizable in the beard (*virtus enim in barba intelligitur*); others saw in it an interpretation of Verse 27 in Genesis which seemed to imply that the first human beings were sexually indistinguishable. It was Professor Georges Gaillard, taking a lead from Mérimée, who solved the enigma to the satisfaction of most modern experts. Professor Gaillard suggested that the painter's technique was to apply his colors on a previously dried coating, which he dampened as he went along. Corrections and additions are very difficult to make with this technique. It seems likely that by mistake the artist first placed his bearded Adam on the left of God. He then realized his error. Since in his drawing only the beard marked the difference between man and woman, he tried to turn Adam into Eve by effacing the beard. But the retouching did not hold and a light beard reappeared on Eve's face.

Several of the St. Savin scenes from Genesis have become familiar through reproductions and postcards. Among them is the Tower of Babel, which is strangely realistic, with medieval masons handing the blocks of stone to one another. In others God is shown accepting Abel's offering with a benevolent gesture, meanwhile frowning upon a harsh, tense Cain; Noah sleeps off an over-indulgence in wine and Ham, who mocked his father's nudity, is punished while Shem and Japheth cover the old man with a coat; finally, Noah's Ark.

The St. Savin ark is a marvelous creation, worthy of much contemplation: it is a three-decked ship, decorated at one end with a fantastic head, comparable to those which are embroidered on the Bayeux tapestry. Animals crowd the lower stories; Noah and his family are more spaciously established on the top deck. In the painting two giants are shown attempting to do violence to Noah's project: they are either trying to climb onto the Ark or to capsize it. In another picture, Lot is represented expressing his gratitude effusively to his uncle Abraham, who has rescued him from his captors. Lot is one of the most appealing figures in the whole series of paintings.

Who painted the St. Savin frescoes is a question shrouded in darkness. Some scholars have distinguished several hands, even several workshops, in the paintings, although the evidence is far from conclusive. There are qualitative differences in some of the paintings, which may mean that several teams of artists may well have succeeded each other within a brief span of time. The frescoes on the nave have rhythm and sweep, as do the scenes on the porch, but the paintings in the crypt, under the choir, evince traces of awkwardness. The difference between those works in the crypt and the frescoes in the upper part of the central church may be simply the result of the passage of time. The ones in the crypt are believed by some experts to have been done some seventy years after the earliest ones, around the middle of the twelfth century. But even this is a moot point. The opinion of Paul Deschamps that they all must have been accomplished within a quarter of a century, around the year 1100, is the most likely. The lack of space and of light in the crypt must have hampered the artists painting there. In truth, there are many points of similarity in the dresses, in the expression of the faces, and the gestures throughout the frescoes in all the sections of the church, including those in the crypt which depict the martyrdom of St. Savin and St. Cyprian, to whom the church is dedicated. Old chronicles relate that the two men came from near Brescia in Italy. They urged inhabitants of that city to renounce pagan worship, whereupon the mob denounced them to the Roman governor. They were thrown into a fire—but it did not consume them while it reduced to ashes the governor and others. They were thrown to lions—who did nothing but gently lick their feet. An angel advised them to go to the land of the Gauls. Pursuing Romans captured them and cut off their heads. On the spot where they perished miracles occurred. Deaf and blind were healed there.

The church itself was perhaps built by Charlemagne in the years 800 to 810. It is a miracle that the paintings of St. Savin have survived at all, for the abbey was stormed alternately by the English and the French during the Hundred Years' War. The earliest of all the French pictorial achievements, rediscovered after more than seven hundred years, they hold a magnificent place in the range of mural art. Henri Focillon may once again be quoted: "French painting anticipates Italian art in the synthesis which the latter will reach only at the end of the thirteenth century, in uniting popular ardor, respect for moral values and the poetics of great form."

THE LAST DAYS OF SAINTS SAVIN AND CYPRIAN. The frescoes in the crypt, situated under the choir, show episodes during the martyrdom of the saints whose relics were venerated in the church. According to tradition they were put to death by their persecutors *(below)* not very far from where the church stands. But before they died they were subjected to many tortures including that of the wheel *(at right)* which is here evoked with a realism that has stirred the emotions of pilgrims for more than 800 years. Finally the two saints were beheaded.

THRUST TO THE HEAVENS

GOTHIC
CHURCHES

Few words have ever been so ineptly chosen as "Gothic"—and few now prove to be so indispensable. All attempts to replace it with a more appropriate term have been in vain. Men of the Middle Ages surely never called their cathedrals "Gothic," since the word was derogatory: it meant barbaric, irregular to the point of ugliness. It was invented by Italian humanists in the latter stages of the Renaissance to express their contempt for the "maniera gotica," an art form taken to have been practiced by Vandals or Goths and guilty of violating the ancient canons of beauty. Unfortunately the use of that adjective influenced people for two hundred years. It kept them from looking sympathetically, or even objectively, at the monuments which they passed daily in Paris, Chartres, Cologne, Salisbury. Racine, going through Chartres, dryly commented, "The Cathedral of Chartres is large, but a little barbaric." Molière, whose comic inspiration owed much to the popular farce inherited from earlier eras and was close to the people, wrote a very bad poem to praise one of his artist friends; in it he spoke contemptuously of everything Gothic:

> "Le fade goût des ornements gothiques,
> Ces monstres odieux des siècles ignorants
> Qui de la barbarie ont vomi les torrents."

> "The insipid taste of Gothic ornaments,
> Those loathsome monsters of ignorant centuries
> Which vomited the torrents of barbarity."

The Jesuit Dictionary of Trévoux, in the eighteenth century, tersely equated Gothic with "coarse" and added: "Gothic architecture is the one most remote from ancient proportions, with no correct profile and no good taste in its chimerical ornaments."

This general scorn for the art of the Middle Ages was supplemented by a number of attempts by architects and ecclesiastics to "improve" the churches. Mansart, Louis XIV's great architect, prepared a project (which he happily lacked the time to carry out) to Italianize the interior of Notre Dame of Paris with square pillars, colored marbles and other Italian novelties. Another great architect of the time, Robert de Cotte, did away with the medieval choir stalls and put in balustrades. In the age of Voltaire the sculpture of Rheims was called "disorderly."

Our reappraisal of the Gothic counts among the many benefits which we owe to that passionate rediscovery of the Middle Ages, of the Orient, of the poetry of the Bible, of Dante and Shakespeare, which goes by the name of Romanticism. The romantics, if they brought with them a new and much needed relativity in matters of taste, more than once lapsed into excesses and ventured preposterous assertions. Chateaubriand gave credence to the myth that Gothic churches had been inspired by Germanic forests and that their pillars rivaled primeval trees. Victor Hugo raved occasionally when singing the praises of Notre Dame or of the castles on the Rhine, but he was also among the first to proclaim that architecture had been the mistress art, the only complete and most grandiose expression of the Middle Ages. "In the Middle Ages, nothing important was thought by men which was not written by them on stone." Michelet upbraided those thick-skinned moderns who took the stones of those churches to be mere stones and did not feel the sap throbbing through them.

Many a romantic admired Gothic structures for their disorder, their defiance of all constricting rules, for their bold emphasis (as they saw it) on gargoyles and grotesque features and their near-Shakespearian madness without method. The romantics pictured masses of humble people collaborating in erecting the walls and towers and inspiring the sculptors and stained-glass artists.

Some of that declamatory and often nationalistic tone has lingered, in Germany and France, in several works treating of Gothic cathedrals. One such work, by the great sculptor Auguste Rodin, whose "Gates of Hell," and "Calais Burghers" recall the tension created by Gothic sculptors, makes statements like these: "The whole of France is present in her cathedrals, just as the whole of Greece is, in an abridged form, in the Parthenon. . . . French cathedrals were born of French nature. The air of the French sky, at once light and gentle, bestowed their grace upon our artists and refined their taste."

For a long time, the Germans insisted upon seeing their ancestors as the originators, if not of the ogive itself, at least of the spirit which made Gothic or ogival architecture possible. Long before Hitler's time, some degree of racism infected a number of German scholars. As respected an art theorist as Wilhelm Worringer, who wrote extensively on Gothic art in the years 1908 to 1924, asserted that "the tendency toward the Gothic appears only where Germanic blood happens to have blended with that of other European races." The Celts and the Romans had a share in that style, he conceded; but "the Germans are the 'sine qua non' condition of the Gothic." Again: "France created the most beautiful and the most alive of Gothic buildings, but not the purest. The country of pure Gothic civilization is the Germanic north."

But those scholars who argue that Gothic belongs to one country or to another forget that frontiers were not, in the Middle Ages, the boundaries that they have since become. The allegiance of artists, and of other men, was not to their native land, but to their patron, or to their team, or to the ecclesiastical chapter which called for their services and rewarded them. They traveled far and wide. An Italian could come and work in France, as Leonardo and Il Rosso did. A Fleming who had settled in France, like Philippe de Champaigne, became a French artist. Jean de Bologne, born in Douai, trained in Antwerp, became a Florentine artist and italianized his name. The Channel constituted no barrier to England for masons and carvers from Normandy. What is beyond dispute is this: A great creative era, between 1150 and 1350, expressed itself in one of the boldest thrusts ever attempted to exalt man and bring him nearer to the divine in its architecture, its sculpture and its stained glass. Music, rich as we know it to have been in the Middle Ages in France, and literature (the stately cathedral-like epic by Dante excepted) did not approach the variety, the subtlety, the grandiose simplicity of medieval architecture, which Rodin called "the most cerebral and the most sensitive of the arts." The Greeks had achieved in their temples marvels of horizontal harmony; they humanized gods into idealized human beings. Gothic architecture stands as the most splendid tribute to man's urge toward exalted elevation.

The transition from Romanesque to Gothic architecture was gradual; it did not occur at the same time in the several countries where Gothic art thrived, or even in the different provinces of one country. It did not even affect different parts of a building simultaneously. Romanesque art survived in Germany down into the thirteenth century; it lingered at least as late in Spain. In Italy, Gothic never put down genuine roots. In France, Gothic flourished most brightly and earliest where Romanesque churches had been least numerous and least striking, in the northern region of the country. It spread most easily where the supremacy of the monarchy was most assured. Security conditions had improved, or at any rate a feeling of security was shared by more people as the feudal system and chivalry had become more firmly established. Hence the need for massiveness and for strong walls with only few openings, which had been a factor in Romanesque construction, was no longer a controlling factor. The new type of church could be less static, and yield to the aspiration for ascending spires and pillars. Everywhere a desire for more light and luminous windows was manifest.

The innovations which eventually, when added to one another, characterized the Gothic style were probably first developed more or less simultaneously by anonymous artisans in widely separated building yards. Exact dates are misleading because they may indicate only when a church was first started, or when it was consecrated; but churches were often finished only after long delays—in the case of German cathedrals like Cologne, after the lapse of no less than five hundred years. English art historians distinguish neatly between their Norman style (up to 1150), their Early English, Decorated English, Perpendicular English and Tudor, each of which covers approximately a century, up to 1550.

In France, Gothic style is taken to have originated at St. Denis, in the choir, around 1140: the abbey was rebuilt in the early 1130's after a fire, and consecrated in 1144. Senlis, Noyon and the splendid cathedral of Laon, which was to be much admired and imitated by German builders, came next. Then, Paris, Chartres and Bourges, begun in the very last years of the twelfth century. Rheims and Amiens followed. The Sainte-Chapelle, Beauvais, Cologne, Strasbourg, Uppsala and Siena were all started between 1227 and 1250.

By the end of the century the splendid creative élan had spent itself. Why? We are left to conjecture. Some reasons have been suggested. It is too easy to argue that the Gothic master builders became too rash and aimed at edifices too gigantic and too lofty. Viollet-le-Duc doubted very much that even Beauvais, whose choir collapsed in 1284, was necessarily doomed to that fate: mistakes in the laying out of the foundations or in building processes had been committed there. It is uncertain whether economic motives, such as the excessive and ruinous expenses entailed by the tall structures of Beauvais and Siena, prevented their completion. A shortage of funds has seldom stopped sovereigns and peoples from indulging luxurious ambitions or a craving for expensive wars.

Our grandfathers thought they had found a comforting explanation of the growth and decline of a style or of an art form in the notion of evolution: tragedy, fiction, satire, opera, Gothic or classic art—all were likened to organisms which grew, reached an ideal point of maturity, then aged, declined and died. But the analogy is unconvincing. It often happens that a new style and those who uphold it come long before the previous one has begun to decline; in fact, the new form frequently comes along when the old one is standing at the very peak of its innovations. In artistic and intellectual matters, if not in political ones, the winning causes are sometimes those which are deserted. Then nothing fails like success.

It is clear today that the provinces surrounding Paris, Ile-de-France, Picardy, and Beauce were the nucleus from which Gothic architecture radiated; the most admired of the Gothic churches are located there. It is most probable, however, that at least one of the characteristic components of the Gothic style, the rib vault, first appeared at Durham in Britain between 1093 and 1104, and that the choir transept of Durham gained a lightness therefrom which contrasted with the massive, inert walls of previous churches. But a style is a spirit, a complex whole and cannot be restricted to one innovation, however important: the use made of such an innovation by those who realize and fulfill its potentialities often becomes as creative as the discovery of the original technical novelty. It is possible, therefore, that the Anglo-Norman builders of Durham, and the Lombard masons who may have anticipated them in groping toward an ogival vault, might have merely attempted an innovation the significance of which they did not understand, and that might not have been important if they had not been followed by the architects of St. Denis, of Senlis, Noyon and Laon.

Histories of architecture, the most succint and the best in English being that of Nikolaus Pevsner, agree on the three chief technical characteristics of Gothic architecture: the pointed arch, the rib vault and the flying buttress. But Pevsner rightly warns that the technical advantages of those innovations, once much exaggerated by French art historians from Viollet-le-Duc to his late nineteenth century followers, were secondary to something else: to "the combination of these motifs for a new esthetic purpose." That old foe of early Christian art, fire, which had consumed so many basilicas with wooden carpentry, had to be vanquished by new devices: first came the massive Roman vault, too ponderous and making for darkness, and the Byzantine cupola, best adapted to a church constructed on the Greek plan, or to the transept cross of a Latin church, or to a baptistery. Several types of vaults were experimented with by Romanesque builders: but it was soon obvious that the weight of the vault had to be counterbalanced by the resistance of the walls, which tended to be pulled apart and had to be supported by pillars. The oblong Gothic vault made it possible to dispense almost entirely with wooden centering underneath and hence decreased the danger of fire. The pointed arch provided the architect with the opportunity to strive for the verticality which was then eagerly desired. To the Gothic mind, as John Harvey has put it, this arch symbolized "the whole of the reawakened, quickened life of the twelfth century, the principle of research, the eager acceptance of new ideas . . . and the establishment of a new conception of humanity, a new ideal." The flying buttress, striding over the collaterals, strengthened the central nave and offset the weight of the high vaulting. It appeared relatively late, and its use was not universal. It was widely criticized; Ernest Renan, who was born in the shadow of the Breton cathedral of Tréguier, ironically compared the Gothic church with its outside carapace to "an animal which carries its skeleton on the outside." Controversies have raged over the first appearance of the ogive, or reinforcing arch of the vault, as they have on the original meaning of the word itself. It was first used in the middle of the thirteenth century in Villard de Honnecourt's album. Ogive has been taken by some to come from the Latin verb "augere," to increase, since it increased the strength of the walls by dividing the weight pressing upon them; by others, it is believed to have come from the French word for trough, "auge," because of the shape. A theory advanced by Viollet-le-Duc stressed the rational character of Gothic building, the close interdependence of all the elements, and the functionalism of that architecture in which the ogival arch acted as an indispensable prop and the buttresses supported the walls as "épaulements." But a French engineer, Victor Sabouret, and an architect, Pol Abraham, challenged what they termed Viollet-le-Duc's "medieval rationalism." They argued that both the ogive and the buttress were mere ornaments, that their role was in no way a functional one, but was one of illusionism. Time has borne them out. In some cases, indeed, as the destruction wrought during two World Wars showed, the structures effortlessly survived the loss of those supposedly essential props.

The beauty of Gothic, for modern admirers of the art, consists first in a harmonious correspondence between the edifice and the site, a harmony not unworthy of the builders of Greek temples. Many a Gothic church, built either in the center of a town or near its ramparts, appears to keep watch over it. Next comes the luxuriance of the art, its audacity in throwing its spires, turrets and nave upward. But the virtues which are sometimes called classical are no less obvious in Gothic art: the ability to organize, to simplify, to control the luxuriance of the sculpture with rigor, to mold light through the stained glass and the many apertures, to make order an integral part of beauty. The profusion of chapels, of statues, of individual masterpieces achieved by sculptor and painter under the controlling guidance of "the master of those who work"—which the word "architect" suggests—all these in no way detract from the overarching order.

A last question must needs be asked. In what relation does Gothic architecture stand to the religious spirit of the Middle Ages at their "top of sovereignty," to use Keats' noble phrase? A convenient contrast was proposed by Viollet-le-Duc. He maintained that, while Romanesque architecture was steeped in faith and was especially remarkable in the abbeys constructed by regular religious orders, Gothic art was secular, or even independent from the church, and was the work of the communes and of the rising middle class. This contention hardly appears tenable today. Those great cathedrals were built amid great impulses of religious faith. We know of some cases, in twelfth century northeastern France, where groups of laymen came together to confess and repent their sins and, as an atonement for them, carted corn, wine, wood and stones to help build their church. The legate Odo of Châteauroux could write: "It is with the farthings offered by old women that Notre Dame of Paris was in large part erected." Large gifts were solicited from the king and the nobility; the canons offered statues or stained-glass windows; funds were raised through relics.

But there was in truth an ardent élan of faith among the small people which sustained the builders and the carvers. In an age when invasions, wars, feuds unleashed many an impulse to destroy, religious faith, if it may be blamed for what was regrettable in the Crusades, also incited men to become creators instead of destroyers.

THE CATHEDRAL OF ST. ETIENNE

BOURGES

The cathedral of Bourges is situated in the geometric center of France, some one hundred and forty miles from Paris. Away from the main arteries which take travelers to Normandy, Brittany, the Basque region, and Provence, it is less often visited by the casual tourist than other great Gothic shrines. Yet it yields to none in variety, nobility and beauty. Many of its features are beyond compare in Western Europe: the Last Judgment sculpted on its central portal, several of its stained glass windows, its apse viewed from the outside, its curious crypt. Aldous Huxley has called it "the grandest, the most strangely and fabulously beautiful building in Europe."

The cathedral rises in the center of a city with a long and rich history. On this site, according to Gregory of Tours, stood the palace of Leocadius, first senator of Gaul. Earlier, there may have been a Roman church on the same spot. In pre-Roman times, Bourges, rising on the slope of a hill surrounded by two small rivers and many brooks and marshes, bore the name of Avaric, which meant "a place with abundant waters." Julius Caesar described the settlement as "the largest and best fortified of the country of the Bituriges."

After the early thirteenth century, the glorious era in which the cathedral was built, the city went through periods of glittering artistic magnificence. Between 1360 and 1416 a younger son of King Jean le Bon, Duke Jean of Berry, brought many decorators, painters and sculptors there. One of them, Paul de Limbourg, was the creator of the famous "Très Riches Heures du Duc de Berry," now at the Chantilly Museum near Paris. During the Hundred Years' War, the Duchy of Berry escaped being conquered by the English; as a result, after King Charles VII of France had lost most of the rest of his kingdom, he was derisively called "the King of Bourges," since that was all he had left. In 1463 Louis XI, who had been born in Bourges, established a university there. The celebrated jurist, Jacques Cujas, taught law in that school in the sixteenth century. Calvin studied there, perhaps associating with German students who may have introduced him to Luther's new ideas.

Unlike the Cistercian monasteries which were built in isolated regions, churches and cathedrals were usually erected in the very midst of busy cities. Artisans' shops and modest houses often rose in their shade, as if to stress that every man should turn to religion at every move in his life. So Bourges was intimately associated with the daily lives of the inhabitants, who entered the churches not only to pray for salvation or to unburden their souls, but also to ask for good health, for rain for their crops, or for success in their commercial enterprises.

How Bourges was built, and by whom, we can today surmise with some certainty, thanks to assiduous research in archives undertaken in England by D. Knoop and G.P. Jones ("The Mediaeval Mason"), in France by Pierre du Colombier ("Les Chantiers des Cathédrales"). Some of the most remarkable studies of French medieval architecture have been those done by American scholars since 1930: by K.J. Conant at Cluny, Charles Seymour at Noyon, Sumner Crosby at St. Denis, Robert Branner at Bourges. But no amount of factual knowledge can reveal to us *why* people built cathedrals, and what they most admired in them. Nor do we know why, after the extraordinary flowering of the twelfth and thirteenth centuries, the inventiveness of the builders suddenly flagged. Certainly the faith of the people did not suddenly vanish in the age of Joan of Arc and of François Villon. The disruption of such historical events as the Hundred Years' War did not impede the development of other arts, such as sculpture and painting. The introduction of Roman law into medieval society, late in the thirteenth century, cannot be blamed; it had no sudden effect on either the faithful majority or the artistic minority.

To be sure, the first evidences of the Renaissance were apparent long before the conventional dates assigned to the beginning of the Renaissance in France, in the middle or late fifteenth century. With its return to an interest in ancient mythological subjects, the Renaissance was to separate the educated classes from a populace long accustomed to imagery drawn from the Scriptures and the lives of the Saints. Still, the first signs of the Renaissance can hardly have been perceptible to the people as a whole. The truth is that no great artistic or literary achievement emerged in Italy after Michelangelo, or in Holland after Rembrandt, or in Spain after Velasquez or Góngora, or in Gothic architecture after Beauvais or Rouen, and we are at a loss to explain why. All we know is that in certain ages, in certain countries, religious feeling expressed itself in magnificent structures which move us to wonder to this very day. Other peoples, probably equally fervent in their cult of the Virgin or in their devotion to Christ the Redeemer or in their fear of the Devil, remained uncreative.

The Bourges Cathedral—or, to call it by its proper name, the Cathedral of St. Etienne—was most probably begun in 1195. Its construction may have been decided upon some ten years earlier, perhaps shortly after the church which had preceded it was destroyed by fire. The choir and the ambulatory were ready by 1214. The structure must have been completed by about 1266. The portals and their sculptures date from the first quarter of the fourteenth century. The cathedral was consecrated in 1324 by Archbishop Guillaume de Brosse.

Although the crypt at Bourges may have been influenced by Notre Dame, it is a moot point whether the cathedral itself owed much to the older Paris structure. The Cathedral of St. Etienne was begun when Henri de Sully, scion of an illustrious family of Sully-sur-Loire, was archbishop (1183-1199). His brother, Eudes de

SQUAT AND STURDY. Seen from its gardens, the Cathedral of St. Etienne at Bourges *(below)*, all burly in its muscular shoulders of sustaining flying buttresses, impresses mainly by its posture of strength. There is nothing of the delicacy and grace that mark the outer ribbings of other Gothic cathedrals. The south tower, called the Deaf Tower because it has no bells, fades off into unimportance in the background.

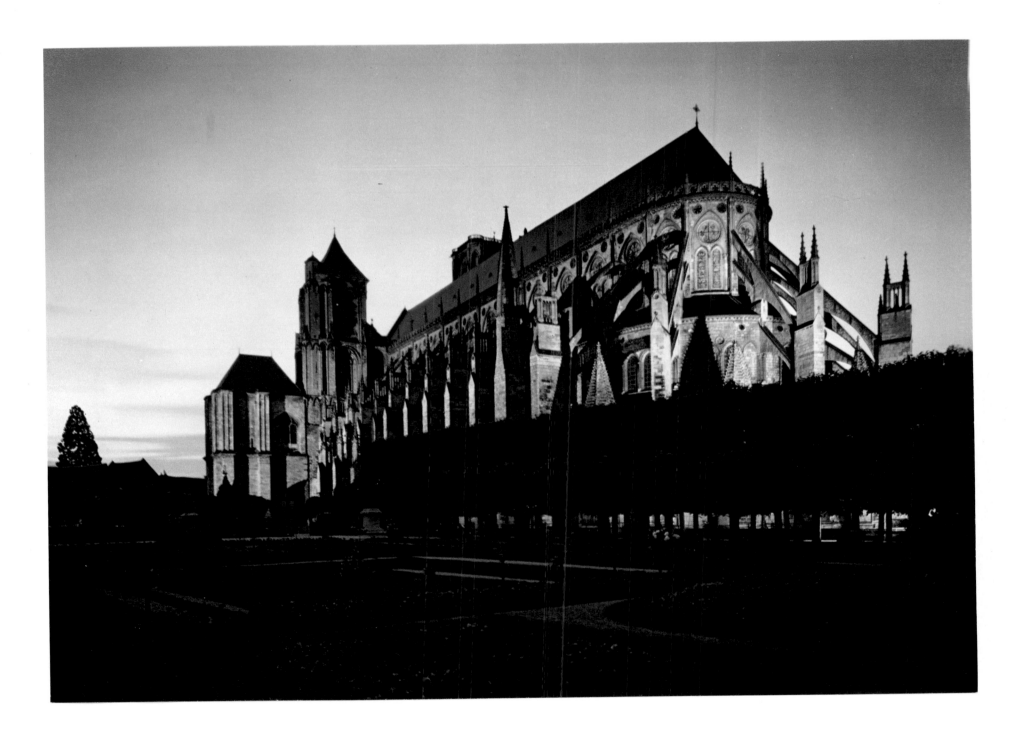

THE GREAT CENTRAL AISLE. The whole nave of St. Etienne gives itself to a visitor in the blink of an eye. Pillars washed by the sun support the high arches called ogives and help create zones of light and shadow that move and flicker—and almost seem to sing.

Sully, became bishop of Paris in 1196 and was in close touch with another bishop of the same name, Maurice de Sully, who had begun Notre Dame around 1163. However, there is no evidence that Henri de Sully selected his architect from among the builders of the Paris cathedral. According to Robert Branner, the architect's influence at Bourges was weaker than that of the chapter which approved the projects for building, fixed the programs for the sculpture and the decoration and engaged the masons. The vastness of the cathedral may have resulted from a desire to outdo similar cathedrals elsewhere, or perhaps this aspect—as well as the lack of transept and the later addition of radiating chapels—was merely a logical development of Gothic architecture at its most fertile stage. The chief builder, whose name we do not know, proved to be a man of genius. The successor to Henri de Sully was Archbishop Guillaume (1199-1210), a man of impressive piety and vast learning. He was preparing, somewhat reluctantly, to depart for the Crusade against the Albigenses in 1210 when he caught cold at a service in the cathedral and died. Miracles were persistently attributed to his relics and in 1218 he was canonized.

The characteristic features of the St. Etienne Cathedral are its immensity and its height; the splendor of its long perspective, unbroken by galleries; its magnificent unity, which should have enraptured Henry Adams, that admirer of the organic unity of medieval churches; and what Henri Focillon has called its "unique personality." The architect was able to do away with galleries, which until then were necessary in any building that rose very high, through full utilization of exterior buttresses. Thus he was able to replace galleries with a triforium, an arcade opened to permit the entry of light. There are no galleries at Chartres, either. The beauty of Chartres lies in part in its strangeness—each side of the transept constitutes a nave by itself and the cathedral makes the most of the variety and even the autonomy of each of its component parts. But the uniqueness of Bourges lies in its classical unity. Indeed, even more than Notre Dame of Paris, it may be asserted that St. Etienne of Bourges —with its double aisles, its double ambulatory (similar to the one in Paris), its sexpartite vaults, its perfect balance between the verticalism of the arcade and the horizontal perspective—stands at the summit of the classicism of the Middle Ages. As Viollet-le-Duc asserts: "the masonry lives, acts, fills a function; it is never a passive or inert mass."

Dmitri Kessel's photographs, taken with great difficulty from a most unusual angle, convey details of the nave, the luminous delicacy which brings out the intentions of the great moulder of space who built it, and the very special combination of columns, capitals, windows and intervals of space—all of which are in accord with the definition of classical beauty as "fitness expressed." The architect sedulously avoided crushing the visitor

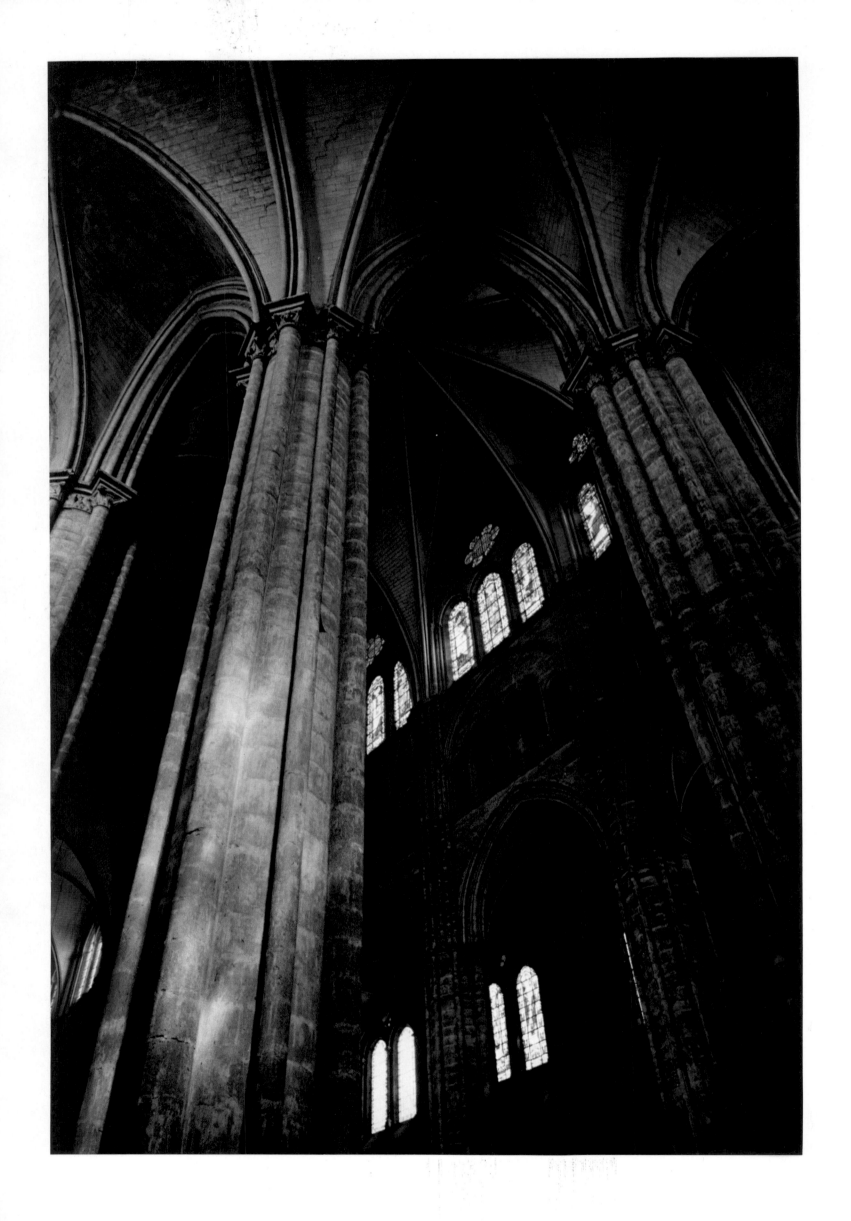

with an overwhelming impression of colossal magnitude. The arcades are tall indeed, with piers rising to sixty feet. But as Robert Branner has pointed out, each of the elements is on a human scale and, as in Baudelaire's "forest of symbols," seems to observe man with a familiar and humane gaze. The height of the nave, however, with an esthetic tension which has been likened by Nikolaus Pevsner to a Bach fugue, carries the eye in an upward thrust which exalts the visitor's sense of loftiness, evoking an almost mystical emotion. Yet in the age when Gothic cathedrals were being erected, men were already speaking against the "disease of building" ("morbus aedificandi"), especially the tendency to raise the chevets or heads of cathedrals too high. Pierre le Chantre, of the chapter of Notre Dame of Paris, was incensed by the overweening ambition he detected in this trend. "The chevets of our churches," he declared, "should be more humble than their bodies, because of the mystery they symbolize. For Christ, who is at our head—the head of this church—is more humble than His church. Yet today chancels are built higher and higher."

The length of the nave at Bourges is slightly less than that of Paris and notably less than those of Rheims and Amiens. The height, on the other hand, is greater than that of Notre Dame and approximately equal to that of Rheims; Amiens and, of course, Beauvais, rose higher.

Part of the special quality of St. Etienne lies in its five naves, spreading over the whole length of the structure, supported by four rows of sixty columns, flooded with a soft, equally distributed light. The only other thirteenth century churches built in this manner, without transepts, are those at Meaux and Mantes. The radiating chapels at Bourges were added after the original construction was completed, probably at the request of the chapter, as the worship of saints, each with his own chapel, spread among the faithful. The crypt, which is admired by all visitors to Bourges, was very skillfully conceived as an artistic solution to a very special difficulty encountered by the builders: the church lies astride a hill and the ground slopes down to the east and west; a substructure was needed, and this was provided by the crypt. Even so, however, the north tower of the cathedral collapsed in 1506 and had to be rebuilt. The five portals in front of the cathedral, corresponding to the five naves, have been universally praised for their stately grandeur. Of unequal height, they avoid too marked a regularity. They are framed by two towers, also happily dissymmetric. One, because it has no bell, is called the Deaf tower; the other one is the Butter Tower, perhaps because it was erected through the gifts of those who were granted dispensations to eat butter and drink milk during Lent in exchange for their donations.

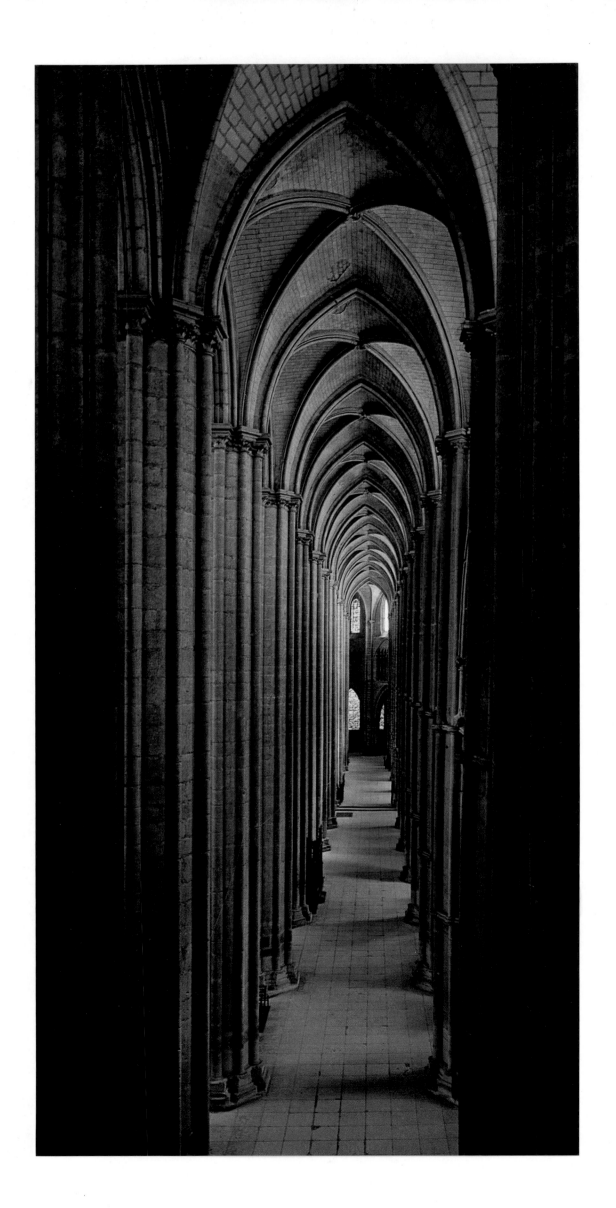

DOWN A SIDE AISLE. In Gothic cathedrals the structure rises more boldly and the side aisles are higher and brighter than in Romanesque churches. Through the radiant filters of the stained glass windows at the left the sun projects fugitive stains of mingled blues and reds on the pillars and into the high vaults.

THE FAMOUS WINDOWS. The Window of the Apocalypse is at the right; on page 154 is a detail from it showing God sitting in judgment as described by St. John: "and out of his mouth went a sharp two-edged sword: and his countenance was as the sun shineth in his strength." On page 155 is a detail from the window of Lazarus.

154

The sculpture on the portals at Bourges has a resplendent beauty. On the right is the portal of St. Ursinus, the first Bishop of Bourges, showing him evangelizing the city on a mission entrusted to him by St. Peter. Next is the portal of St. Etienne, with a modern statue of the patron saint of the cathedral. At the farthest left, the portal of another bishop of Bourges, St. Guillaume, shows him helping the poor, healing the sick, and exorcizing a man possessed by a demon, who has appeared in the shape of a wolf. The portal of the Virgin had to be reconstructed after the north tower collapsed in 1506. On the tympanum of that portal are sculptured scenes of the Assumption and of the Crowning of the Virgin; a curious feature is that here the rule which usually has the Virgin seated on Christ's right is broken.

Most famous of all is the central portal, the portal of the Last Judgment. It must have been done around 1275 and it ranks among the masterpieces of Gothic sculpture. The theme is a common one in medieval art: the dead arise, lifting the covers of their graves to implore the heavens; Archangel Michael holds his scale and weighs the souls, directing the elect to the right, toward Abraham's bosom, the damned to the boiling kettles of Hell. The gentle beauty of St. Michael's face gives it a place among the most touching angelic images in Gothic art. The picture of those who are doomed to eternal punishment is strikingly eloquent. Some of them have human heads drawn on their abdomens to symbolize their greed: they have placed themselves at the service of their lowest appetites. A bishop and a king are among those who are thrown into the gaping mouth of a monster (the Leviathan from the Book of Job); snakes and toads devour them. Among the blessed, welcomed by St. Peter and by angels who prepare crowns for them, are a friar and a king, perhaps St. Louis. Christ is depicted full face, seated on His throne, raising His hands to display the scars left by the Nails. His open tunic reveals the wound in His side. Flanking him are angels carrying a number of holy and sacred objects: the Cross, the Crown of Thorns, the Spear and the Nails.

Emile Mâle, the most admired writer on medieval iconography, has analyzed this central portal of Bourges in his "Religious Art of the Thirteenth Century." He found virtually nothing among other examples of Gothic sculpture to match this most awesome and masterful portrayal of the dead arising to life, snatched from a wily and envious Satan by St. Michael—a theme that derives from the "psychopompos" Hermes (that is, Hermes the conductor of souls) and from Egyptian sculptures, which also depict the weighing of souls. It is, Mâle, wrote, "the most splendid of our sculpted Last Judgments" with the risen dead "dazzled by the full light of Eternity."

156

PORTALS OF MAJESTY. The central entrance to St. Etienne is a masterwork of medieval sculpture. From a pedestal Christ the Teacher welcomes the faithful to the church. In the panel above him the dead arise from their graves; above this panel is one in which St. Michael the Archangel stands ready to weigh the sins of man. At the summit Christ appears again, now as a stern judge to pass judgment on all souls while the Mary and St. John beseech His mercy.

The stained glass at St. Etienne ranks with the sculpture of the porch. The five chapels of the apse have medallion windows, dating from 1215-1225, in glowing deep blue and red. The most striking, however, are those of the choir, which span three centuries. Those from the thirteenth century are the most vivid in their contrasting colors, those from the fourteenth are notable for their similarity to well-organized pictures, those dating from the fifteenth are without par in that century. The emphasis is on the Virgin (in the aisle and the main clerestory) and on stories from the Old and the New Testament: the Joseph stories, Lazarus, Christ seated on the rainbow and surrounded by the twenty-four old men of the Book of Revelation (who were, in medieval times, identified with the Prophets), the episode of the wise and the foolish virgins. The latter, five in number, symbolize the five bodily senses; in medieval theology the wise ones, waiting for the mystical spouse and carrying the lamp burning with love for God, stood for the five senses of the soul and the five forms of inner contemplation. The famed window of the Good Samaritan charmed the people of the Middle Ages through its narrative vividness. The learned men, intent upon symbolic interpretation, read into it far more. For example, as Emile Mâle explained, the traveler on the road from Jerusalem to Jericho stood for the fallen man, for Jericho meant "moon" in Hebrew, and hence called to mind eclipses and failings. The traveler was assisted not by either priest or Levite —who were the Old Law—powerless to cure mankind, but by the Samaritan—the New Law—who tended his wounds after he had been attacked by thieves.

The impact of the marvelous structure of Bourges was felt far and wide in the thirteenth century. Stained glass artists from Bourges, such as Guillaume de Marcillat, were called to Arezzo in central Italy, and elsewhere, to teach their skill; the cathedral of St. Martin of Tours, destroyed by fire in 1202, was rebuilt around 1210 on the pattern of Bourges—that is, with five naves and a double ambulatory (only to be destroyed again after the French Revolution). Burgos in Spain borrowed much from Bourges (as well as from Norman churches) and adapted these borrowings, with dubious success, to Spanish taste. Toledo also offers close similarities to St. Etienne. In France, Le Mans and Coutances, as Robert Branner has shown, reinterpreted with originality some of the features of Bourges. Few great cathedrals exercised such an impact on their age.

Let Marcel Aubert, a learned student of French cathedrals, sum up for us its unique contributions: "By the lightness of its mass, the pyramidal composition of values, the skillful gradation of its upward lines, the cathedral of Bourges is perhaps, of all cathedrals, the one which conveys the most moving impression of Gothic art."

158

THE MINSTER OF OUR LADY

ULM

The church, or minster, of Ulm was never a cathedral, but its architecture is striking, its spire is the highest in Christendom and its wood carvings possess a strange beauty. While it is less famous than other Central European religious edifices, the minster of Ulm is very characteristic of German art of the late Middle Ages—and Germany is, after France and Britain, the region where the Gothic style brought forth the largest number of talents and brilliant creations. For modern minds, which find it hard to divorce art from the social and economic conditions under which it appeared, Ulm offers an added interest: we happen to know something of the architecture and builders of the German church, and thus we have a certain amount of information explaining why it was erected.

It is often suggested by German writers on art as well as on politics and literature that their country and its culture are misunderstood abroad. Although important exceptions to this claim readily come to mind (Goethe and Hegel, for example, have always had numerous admirers abroad, and there have been times when German and Austrian music enjoyed a near monopoly in the programs of symphony orchestras) it has some truth when applied to art. It was not until the exodus in the 1930s of many architects and painters who had been connected with the Bauhaus—an exodus that demonstrated what wealth and fecundity German art had boasted just before World War I and during the Weimar Republic—that there occurred a careful appraisal of what had been most original in that realm in Teutonic lands.

The Germans themselves must be allotted a share of responsibility for the misunderstanding. Until Johann Winckelmann's great work on the art of antiquity in 1764, they had largely ignored the creations of their own artists, turning instead to Greece, Italy or France, and bowing to rules laid down in Paris. It was not until the start of the nineteenth century that Germans began to extol German Gothic, to grant Dürer his full due, and to perceive the architectural originality of their old cities, notably Nuremberg. Thanks to the enthusiasm generated by such romantics as Wilhelm H. Wackenroder and Ludwig Tieck around 1800, a number of religious edifices that had been unfinished for centuries were finally completed; among them were the Cologne cathedral, the Regensburg church, and the church of Ulm, finished between 1844 and 1890.

Germany's location in the center of Europe would seem to have made her an ideal artistic intermediary between East and West: Byzantine and even Scythian influences were indeed felt during the Carolingian period and later, and the miniatures that reached a high degree of refinement in the Ottonian age may have been influenced by Persian models. The claims of the Holy Roman Emperors over the Italian peninsula encouraged

PROUD CHURCH AMONG THE CATHEDRALS. The city of Ulm on the Danube was never the seat of a bishop and thus has never had a cathedral. But in the Middle Ages the town was beautiful and prosperous and its citizens decided to build a church as large and magnificent as many cathedrals. The result is the Minster of Ulm, here seen dramatically illuminated of a summer's night. It was built slowly and with difficulty amid wars and travails; its great spire, the highest in Europe, was completed only in the nineteenth century although the plans for it were drawn up in the fourteenth century. But Ulm always had good architects and fine sculptors and they made a lovely church.

163

close contacts with Italian art, and Cluny and the Cistercian monasteries introduced many a French model into the empire. Romanesque art, which developed with surprising speed in France, spread more slowly in German lands. In Germany Romanesque art resisted the advent of the new, or Gothic, style with more stubbornness. Thus the Romanesque style survived in Germany until late into the thirteenth century. Among the noteworthy examples of German Romanesque are Speyer, St. Maria im Kapitol and Hildesheim.

When Gothic art did penetrate into Germany, it blended with Romanesque features and thus took on a distinctive appearance. Some traits of the French Gothic, such as the buttress, were not easily naturalized, but the rib vault and the ogival arch soon assumed a special Germanic character. The admirable west front of the French cathedral of Laon, with its two tall towers, and other towers on the transept fronts, served as a model for several German churches—for example, Bamberg and Naumburg—but these influences would hardly be worth mentioning if they had merely led to slavish imitation. Such was not the case in Germany, which, in the thirteenth and fourteenth centuries, displayed an incredible eagerness to build and to carve stone and wood. Ulm is one of several churches in southern Germany that stand as outstanding examples of a Gothic architecture that had assimilated the lessons of its French precedents with creativity and independence.

Ulm is an ancient medieval city on the left bank of the Danube, between Stuttgart and Strasbourg on the west, Nuremberg, Bamberg and Bayreuth on the north or northeast, and Augsburg and Munich on the southeast. It was once a "free city" and it enjoyed an active municipal and commercial life. One of Napoleon's most famous victories over the Austrians, immediately preceding that of Austerlitz, took place there in 1805; as one consequence there is a commemorative Rue d'Ulm in Paris, just as there is a Waterloo Street in London.

The church of Ulm was started in 1377. It was intended to be a cathedral—that is, to be the church of a bishop—but never became one. The building underwent a number of modifications. In 1392 it was decided to make the plans much more ambitious than they originally were, and Ulrich von Ensingen, the first member of a dynasty of three architects, took over the enlargement of the building. Von Ensingen, who had worked in Milan, started the ambitious tower in front and the porch underneath.

Although the entire city then numbered barely more than 12,000 inhabitants, the church was planned to hold at least double that number. The spire, its tip rising over three elegant tiers, reaches a height of about 530 feet, 15 feet higher than the Cologne tower, the next highest in Europe. The long nave, the two minor

PROPHET. Hans Multscher carved the statue of Moses at left, one of those that decorate the tabernacle of the Ulm church. The tabernacle, made in 1467, is constructed in the form of a miniature cathedral.

PROPHETESS. In the Middle Ages it was believed that pagan prophetesses called sibyls had announced the coming of Christ. They are sculptured in several versions in Ulm; this is a Cimmerian sibyl from the Crimea.

167

towers at the eastern end of the church, and the boldness of the proud spire bestow on the whole structure a majestic appearance; the tower dominates the city to which it brought glory.

Fanatic admirers of French and English Gothic have sometimes objected that the proportions of the church at Ulm are less felicitous than those of their favorite cathedrals at home, but the structure seems to have been first intended to be what the Germans call a "Hallenkirche," a hall church. In that type of church the aisles or "collaterals" are as long and as high as the nave; the pillars are slender and, as the art historian A. E. Brinck-mann puts it, "appear to hang like stalactites." Heinrich Parler, the great Swabian builder who helped plan Ulm, had made the "Hallenkirche" fashionable in Germany, and similar churches also were erected elsewhere. Bristol in England and many refectories in French abbeys were erected on the same pattern.

The Ulm church was, of course, Roman Catholic when it was planned, but it was later taken over by Luther's Reformation and became a place of worship for Protestants. The Ensingen family worked on it between 1392 and 1471; the famous choir stalls were wrought between 1469 and 1474 by Jörg Syrlin the Elder. The construction then underwent many interruptions; the building was repeatedly near the point of being given up altogether before it was finally completed in the nineteenth century.

Informed scholars on German architecture, such as Nikolaus Pevsner, who was educated in Leipzig before he became an English art historian, have attempted to establish a link between the original features of German churches and the Lutheran spirit of German Protestantism. Pevsner wrote: "The discrepancy between interiors of undulating flow, in which the individual may lose himself as between the trees of a forest, and exteriors of power-ful solidity with unbroken walls and two rows of windows, heralds the mood of the German Reformation, torn between mystical introspection and a hearty new thrust into this world." The conjecture is tempting, even if one adds that the combination of mystical piety and of earthly common sense never was the monopoly of one sect or one religious order. The shrewdness of many a mystic has more than once been noticed, admired, and feared.

The original designs for the construction of the Ulm church had been offered by the members of that illustrious family of builders, the Parlers, whose advice had been sought by the burghers of the city. But the magni-ficent nave of the Strasbourg cathedral, begun in the second half of the thirteenth century, and of Cologne—which was started in 1248, set out to rival Amiens, and had its choir completed only in 1322—stimulated the envy of the proud city of southern Germany. Ulrich von Ensingen designed a spire for Ulm similar to Strasbourg's.

But in 1529 the tower of Ulm had to be abandoned. Political conditions had changed. The son and the grandson of Ulrich, Mathäus and Moritz, were not animated by the same fire as their ancestor. They had been entrusted with other construction elsewhere which dissipated their energy. In addition, they may well have felt daunted by the prodigious and somewhat pretentious structure which had been contemplated for the front tower. Indeed, the supporting piers soon showed their inadequacy for any plan so ambitious. Andrew Martindale, the English art historian who has made a close study of the manner in which Gothic cathedrals were built and of their economic and social backgrounds, states that by 1492 the flaws in the structure had caused stones from the tower vault to fall into the church. A new master builder was thereupon consulted; he made the necessary repairs to the structure, but the vaults of the aisles had to be rebuilt. Originally, they had been planned on a huge scale, comparable to those of a "Hallenkirche," but subsequent alterations of the plans and the raising of the central vault to an inordinate height, had weakened the side vaults, the pressure of which was no longer counterbalanced. In 1502, the aisle vaults were done away with, the aisles were divided and two smaller vaults replaced the single large one which the Ensingen family had dreamed of.

These mishaps afford the art historian an advantage of which Martindale has ingeniously availed himself in his research. Very solid and uneventfully completed churches, like Horace's "just and determined man," fear no cataclysm—and, like the proverbial and mythical happy peoples, have no history. But churches whose vicissitudes last over hundreds of years often have many stone doctors called to their wavering sides and nurses brought in to dress their gaping wounds. Hence conferences, consultations and health bulletins are recorded in archives which throw a little light upon one of the darkest mysteries of the past ages: how did masons build in the absence of the elaborate blueprints which modern workmen find indispensable? And in what relation did they stand to church and town councils, in an age when schoolmen and theologians seem to have evinced only scant respect for manual laborers who often could not read and who thought only "with their hands"?

The documents recording the quandary of the Ulm councilmen and their moves to avert the collapse of their ecclesiastical edifice have disappeared. But the missing facts can be deduced, for the archives recording the similar difficulties experienced by the Milan cathedral have remained and have been studied by the modern experts. Milan, like Ulm and Cologne, was not completed until the nineteenth century. Moreover, the committee in charge of completing or of saving the Milan cathedral, begun in 1386, sent consultants to observe the

Germanic achievement: two of the architects of the Ulm church, Heinrich Parler and Ulrich von Ensingen, were among those called to the Lombard city. However, as often happens, the strictures of the consultants irked the consultees. "Truth alone hurts," the old saying goes.

Like Molière's doctors, the Germanic and Gallic master builders diagnosed Milan's disease in conflicting terms; but they united in blaming the inadequate foresight of the Italians, unaccustomed as they were to the requirements of Gothic architecture. The Italians, in their turn, were not ready to confess as Leonardo da Vinci had, "mihi defuit symmetria prisca"— that the symmetry of old had not been recaptured by them. As a result of all the wrangling, irregularities and flaws appear in the Milan church—as they do in the Ulm church as well.

But several features of those buildings command our admiration today. Beauty abounds in the sculpture of Ulm even more than in the architecture. French Gothic sculpture was closely integrated with the church, whether it was on porches and portals, galleries and even buttresses or decorative capitals. German sculpture tended to be independent of the structure it enhanced. But it never lost a down-to-earth quality, even when it appeared to idealize figures such as the famous rider of Bamberg at the entrance of the St. George's choir, who may represent St. Stephen of Hungary. From the statues of Rheims, which some Germanic sculptors had studied, they chose what was closest to their idea of antiquity. But they did not divorce their statuary from the environment and from the soil, as the Greeks often did—even though the splendid Bamberg horseman breathes a noble serenity and a grandiose simplicity not very different from the virtues often lauded in the art of ancient Greece.

Jörg Syrlin the Elder, the sculptor who carved the wooden stalls of Ulm between 1469 and 1474, was also an artist of genius. Among his creations at Ulm is Pythagoras, his curly hair streaming from the cap on his wrinkled brow, the folds of his robe draped as if shivering with the thrills of his inner life; this Pythagoras seems to listen to the music of the spheres which he attempts to echo on the instrument which his right hand plays. Other sculpted stalls, as energetic and refined as the Pythagoras, blend Old Testament personages and scientists or poets from the Greco-Roman world. The geographer Ptolemy watches a globe symbolizing the earth as then known (America was not discovered until about twenty years after the Ulm stalls were carved). Perhaps the most striking of those nobly stylized figures is Vergil, his chin firm, his hands delicate and expressive, his eyes inspired by the vision of the Christian world, yet unborn, which he was credited by the Middle Ages with having heralded in his fourth Eclogue. Samson, holding the lion's jaw in his hand, rapt in tragic sorrow, and Job, lean,

sick and in rags, rank among the most pitiable heads ever sculpted in the Middle Ages. Not all the sculpture
at Ulm is by Syrlin. For example, Moses—tall, eyes downcast, standing as a pensive repository of the trust
of the eternal—was created by Hans Multscher. But all of it has been highly lauded: Wilhelm Pinder, the
German art historian, has said that Ulm's sculpture is a unique mixture of force and delicacy.

The feminine personage of the sibyl haunted Syrlin, the sculptor of the stalls. This ancient prophetess was
honored in the Middle Ages as having announced, in several parts of the pagan world, the advent of the Messiah.
She is sculpted in many Gothic churches of Christendom, for example that of Auxerre in France, and she is called
upon to testify, in the hymn "Dies Irae," to the coming of the wrathful Doomsday. There are varied representations of that strange feminine character in art, and several appear at Ulm. One is the Sibyl of Cimmeria, a pale
and melancholy Oriental woman, her headdress falling over her ears and framing her inspired face, her hands artfully holding her book of Sibylline leaves. Others include the Sibyl of the Hellespont and that of Tibur in Italy,
each displaying a different personality and pose. One of them appears to have been modeled, as stone statues
of saints in German churches often are, on the robust women the sculptor could observe around him.

Sibyls and prophets held a special fascination for medieval artists and for the medieval mind in general.
The prophecies of the Old Testament were believed in literally; they were thought to offer the most convincing
proof of the New. Jonah's three days inside the whale thus forecast the three days which elapsed between the
Crucifixion and the Resurrection of Christ. Jacob preferring his younger son, Ephraim, to the older Manasseh
forecast Christ's preference for the Gentiles over the Jews. In the Middle Ages churches had to be oriented
with their altars to the east but their entrances facing west because Christ, when dying on the Cross, was reported
to have turned His face westward, toward Rome and the Gentiles. The lion held a regal place in the sculptured
ornaments of churches because of the belief that the cubs of that animal were born dead and were brought to
life after three days by a roar from their parents.

Although such symbolism may not seem to the modern mind to constitute evidence, it did in the Middle
Ages—and it provided artists with a treasury of concrete themes for their work. Etienne Gilson, one of the most
profound students of medieval philosophy, wrote of the spirit of those ages (which he is very far from considering
as "dark"): "For a thinker of that time, to know and to explain a thing always consists in showing that it is not
what it appears to be; it stands as a symbol of a deeper reality which it prefigures, or it signifies something else."

172

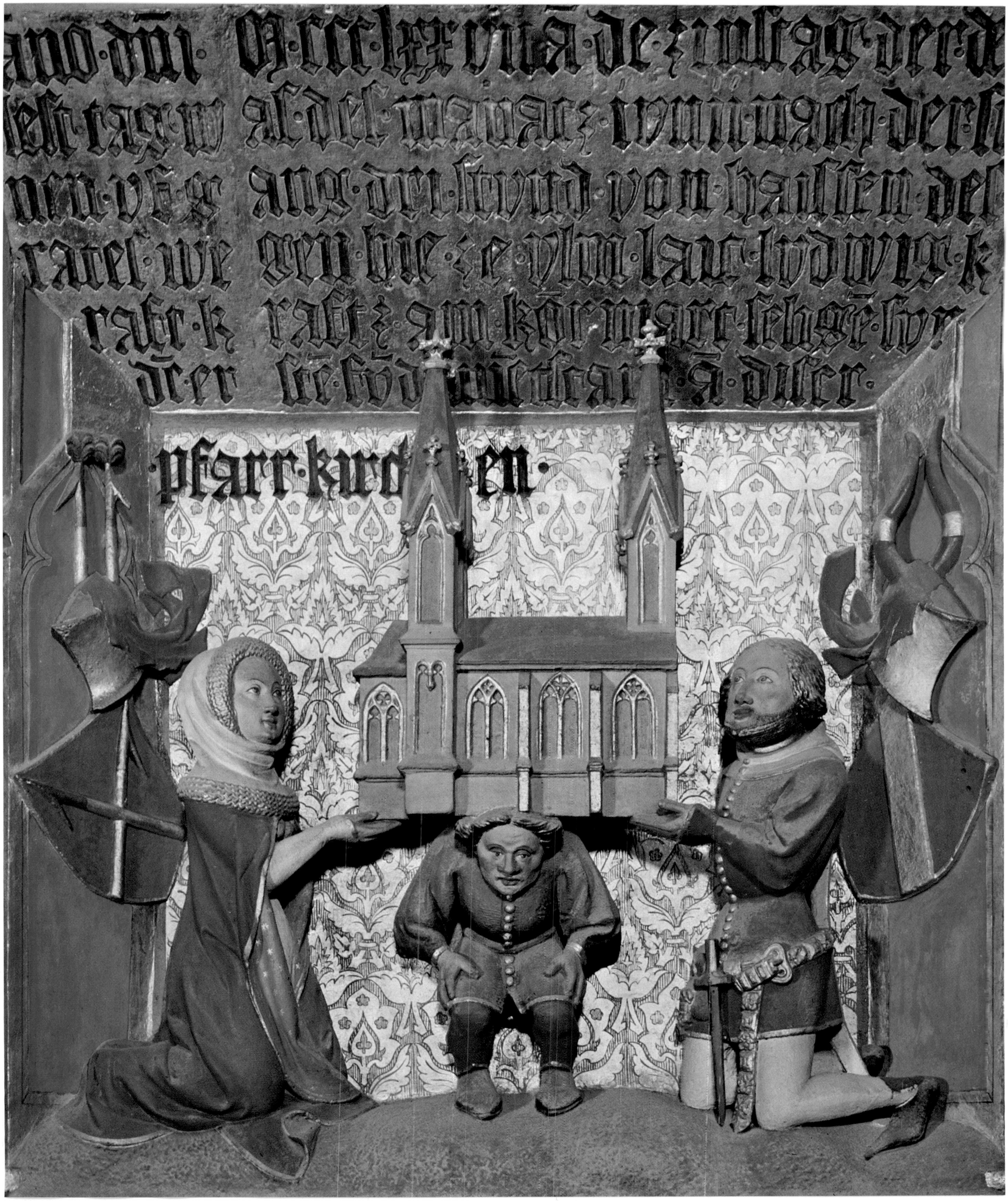

THE CATHEDRAL OF ST. ANDREW

WELLS

A few eminent composers and painters Britain can boast of, but the genius of that nation has never expressed itself in the plastic and pictorial arts, or in music, as superbly as it has across the Channel or in the peninsulas watered by the Mediterranean. And in philosophical speculation, Britain has instinctively eschewed the kind of ambitious metaphysical disquisitions and comprehensive systems which the brutal wind of cold facts might dissolve into "an unsubstantial palace faded." But Britain has been supreme in politics, in science and in poetry. It has also risen high in architecture, the most comprehensive of the arts, which is akin to poetry in the demands it makes upon imagination and in its ascending thrust. Architecture is also close to the scientific spirit, for the builder, the man who undertakes to shape space, must bow to the Baconian precept which warns him that he can command nature only by obeying it. And it is akin also to the art which teaches men, or should teach them, to live together in society and to blend order and progress happily in their social organization. An architect cooperates with other artists: sculptors, engravers, decorators, painters and technicians such as town planners. He also cooperates with the people as a whole for he cannot disregard them in order to embody solitary dreams in stone, any more than a dramatist or composer can. And he can be a precursor only within modest limits; he has to discern and work with the underlying trends of his age which may bring forth the style of tomorrow.

The cathedral at Wells is one of the score of great English cathedrals which have given Britain an eminent place among the countries of the West where Gothic art reached its highest. Durham, Canterbury, Winchester, Lincoln, Salisbury may be better known for artistic or historical reasons. Some rise in a more dramatic setting than Wells. Others were associated with tragic events in the history of Britain, a history which was as turbulent for several centuries as that of the Italian cities which Marlowe, Shakespeare and their contemporaries imagined to be replete with lurid crimes of lust, wrath and jealousy. The proximity of universities to Ely, Exeter and Oxford has enriched these shrines with a treasure of literary associations. In many respects however, Wells ranks among the finest and the most characteristic of the one hundred or so cathedrals of England, partly because the turmoil of history long by-passed that serene district of England, partly because of the harmony of the natural setting.

More than twenty of the cathedrals of England have not survived the wear and tear of time, assisted immeasurably by the destruction of men. From Henry VIII to Cromwell, John Knox and other reformers, before Englishmen mastered the art of agreeing to disagree, they worked as much havoc on their architectural legacy as did the fanatic "friends of man" during the French Revolution. About fifty of the English churches which

THE CATHEDRAL OF WELLS. This famous church, framed in foliage and reflected in a pond, is one of the smallest and loveliest in England. The view here is from St. Andrew's bridge. It shows the cathedral from the back, with its massive central tower, the south part of the transept, the choir, retro-choir and the Lady Chapel.

were once cathedrals (that is, literally, churches which contained the "cathedra" or throne of a bishop) have fallen from high estate or are not in use. Only some twenty-five are still cathedrals today and some of these suffered from the excessive zeal of the Victorian restorers, bent upon making the cathedrals of England close to what they might have been in Gothic times. A boundless love of the medieval past often served nineteenth century artists and restorers no better than it did, say, Walter Scott, Tennyson, or William Morris at their least inspired moments.

How do the English Gothic churches compare with others? Comparisons are difficult to avoid—or make—in a discussion of the ecclesiastical monuments of the Middle Ages. No country then worked in isolation from the others and innovations traveled fast from one building yard to another. Historians, who rarely succeed (and often hardly try) to avoid nationalism, engage in controversies as to the priority of their own countries, nearly a thousand years ago, in introducing the ribbed vault or a certain kind of tower. They weigh the merits of English style against the German or the French.

These debates are not altogether idle. The culture of the West was always nurtured on division, and the overarching unity of Western Europe was made up of diversity. The most national, even the most local of builders, the artists most deeply engrossed in the scene immediately around them and the least cosmopolitan (we can here suggest as examples such widely divergent figures as Bach, Cézanne, William Faulkner) often turn out later to have been the most universal.

John Harvey, author of "The English Cathedrals," stresses the rich diversity of English cathedrals, which exists within a more homogenous ensemble than was known in France, where the number of sees and of cathedrals was incomparably larger. While readily admitting that Chartres, Rheims or Bourges come near to a perfection unequaled in England, he emphasizes the empiricism and the soundness, even homeliness, of the English churches, which do not show the audacious extravagance displayed at Beauvais or Strasbourg. "The English temperament is uneasy upon the heights; at its best it still remains human, not bound to the earth, but firmly rooted in it," he remarks. There have been mystics, idealists, chimerical dreamers in English life; touchingly and admirably unpractical poets, one of whom has been called "an ineffectual angel," as an angel should perhaps best be in a religion where "one thing alone is necessary." But John Harvey may be rightfully proud of what he considers the special quality of the cathedrals of England: they invite the weary to seek repose inside. A meditative poet like George Herbert would indeed feel more at home in Wells Cathedral than a Henry Vaughan exulting that he:

"Saw Eternity the other night,
Like a great ring of pure and endless light."

Some English art historians contend that the very fact that the English church expressed the more empirical temperament which the British attribute to themselves also diminished their grandeur, and endowed them with less intellectual and rationalistic beauty than most of the French cathedrals. The quality of reason has been stressed by the admirers of Notre Dame of Paris and even by those of Chartres more than the quality of charity. Unity, serene harmony, a vision of beauty seen, in Leonardo's words, as a thing of the mind and of the spirit, may indeed be seen to predominate at Chartres and Notre Dame. Prophets after the event are fond of pointing to the latent classicism of these imposing French churches. In contrast, John Harvey insists, the English eschew ruthless logic in art and elsewhere. They evince in their cathedrals the British fondness for "muddling through."

When Anglo-Saxon England was first evangelized by missionaries, it was made up of seven kingdoms, to which historians have affixed the name of "The Heptarchy": Wessex, Sussex, Essex and Kent in the south of the island; East Anglia facing the Low Countries; and farther north, Mercia and Northumbria. After the Norman Conquest, the cathedrals that had been located in small towns were relocated in larger ones. These, like Ely, Lincoln, Norwich and Wells, have ever since been called cathedral cities.

At the outset English cathedrals aimed at length, while the French ones searched for height. But a so-called "Perpendicular" style was eventually developed in England. Originality and audacity are displayed in the disposition of the towers and in the emphasis placed on the sculpture of the lateral porch.

Besides their emphasis on length, the English churches had in common an elaborately developed central tower, a tower at the east which was usually square, and often two towers at the west. Wells is known for its stress on the square, the innovation of the Lady Chapel, the bright light flooding the high altar, the famous curves of the double arches inside and several details of the sculpture.

It has been argued that the square chevet, which is a distinctive feature of English cathedrals, can be ascribed to a lingering pagan influence. According to this theory, the solar worship of the pagans—England remained steeped in pagan traditions much later than continental Europe, down to the ninth century—led the Christian builders to orient their altars more correctly to the east and to adopt a square plan for that purpose. The very special charm of Wells stems from the harmony of the cathedral and of its striking Chapter

THE BROAD AND BUTTRESSED FAÇADE. The imposing front of Wells Cathedral, considered one of the best English Gothic churches, spreads over 140 feet. In niches in the façade are many of the cathedral's 350 surviving statues of saints and notables, many of them no longer identifiable. This massive façade gives the impression that the structure is larger than it truly is. The nave occupies only the area between the towers.

CURVES AND DOUBLE ARCHES. The inverted arches at Wells, serving as buttresses, are found in few Gothic edifices. They were installed at Wells in the fourteenth century when it was discovered that the central tower was too heavy for its footings. As a consequence, the long vista in the nave, much-beloved by English church builders, was lost; but a charming stone pattern was gained.

It also has great historical appeal. It has truly been said: "There is no other place where you can see so many of the ancient buildings still standing and still put to their own use." The beauty of Wells is not that of ruins, but that of the past still present and alive among us.

Wells constituted a difficult and successful experiment. It shook off the remnants of Norman influence and established the early English style in a very pure manner. A linear emphasis is conspicuous. The triforium—the space behind the blank arches below the clerestory, between the roof of the aisles and the vault—forms a continuous line. During the fifteenth century, a gallery was provided in the middle nave below a window on the south, probably to be used by musicians. On one of the arcades, near the west end of the church, the heads of a bishop and a king symbolize church and state to which the citizens had parallel obligations. The southern transept is somewhat heavy; it must antedate the Gothic style of the northern, the style which generally prevails at Wells. The northern transept is elaborately adorned in its upper arcade and the triple lancet windows of some arches. Two chapels occupy the southeast aisle of the transept: they are dedicated to St. Calixtus and to St. Martin of Tours. (One of the early bishops of Wells had come from the French city.) The chapel of St. Martin seems once to have been decorated with frescoes. The tombs of bishops in Wells are especially striking. One, against the south wall, has panels of fine artistry, representing the Annunciation, mourners around the Tomb, and the Holy Trinity. On another, that of William de Marchia, bishop in 1293 and 1302, angels support his head, a dog is at his feet. These funerary monuments are made of limestone from Doulting, a few miles from Wells.

A famous feature, as well as a much debated one as far as the esthetic effect is concerned, is the crossed or inverted arches in the cathedral. These came about because the central tower in the nave gave ominous signs of subsiding, perhaps as a consequence of an earthquake in the middle of the thirteenth century, but more probably after the tower had been heightened by one story and the whole balance upset. An ingenious device, propping the stones beneath the tower with spectacular inverted arches, was resorted to. The whole perspective of the cathedral was thus cut, as it is in other countries by a jube or in Spain by the "capilla major." It may be regretted, but the sagging tower was saved by this and the church was preserved from collapse.

The Lady Chapel is another special element of the Wells edifice. It must have been built around 1320-1325. It began as a separate building, but it was later joined to the church. The space which lies between the Lady Chapel and the choir is known as the retro-choir —or retroquire. Both are very original architecturally,

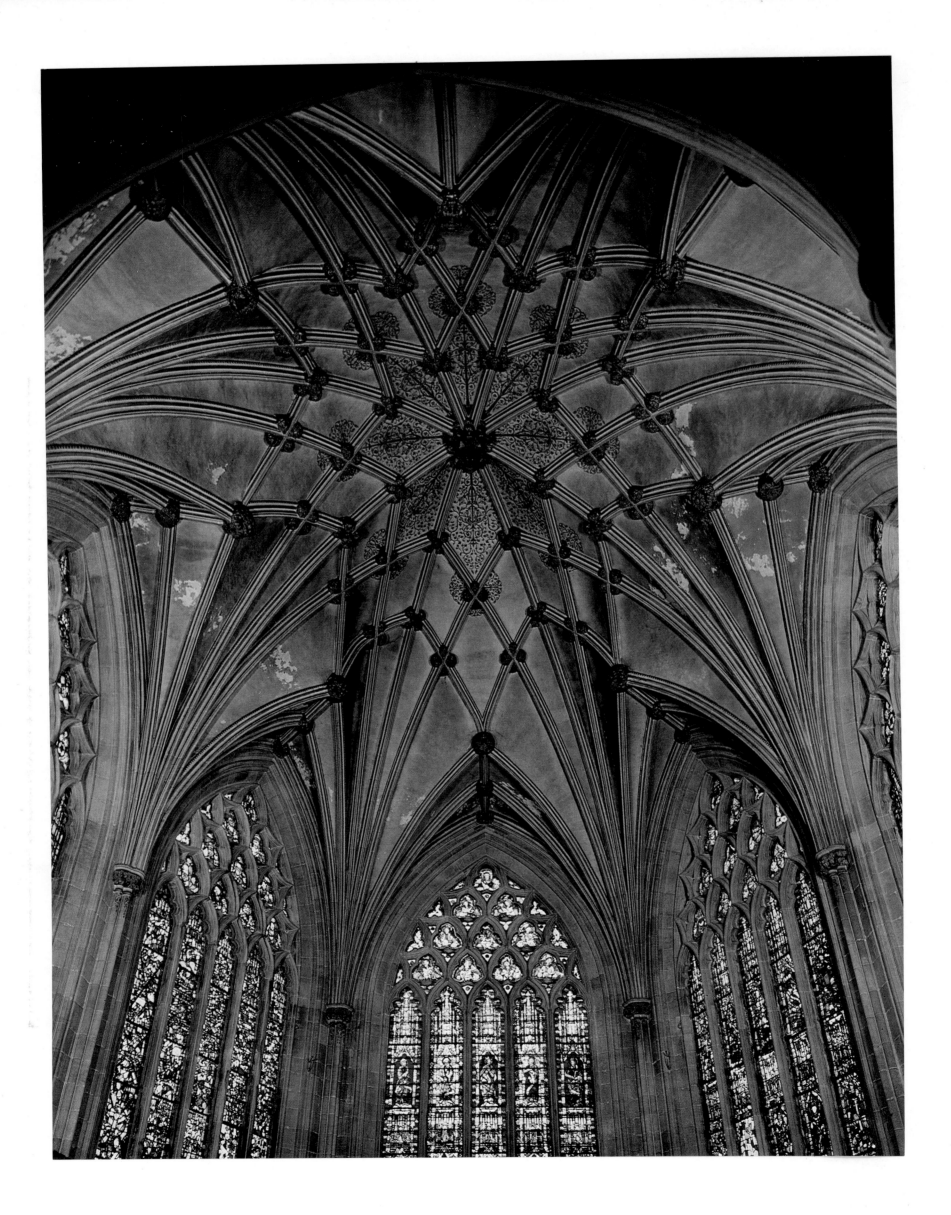

UNDER THE VAULT OF OUR LADY. The Lady Chapel *(left)* was built behind the cathedral early in the fourteenth century and then joined to it by a prolongation of the choir. The vault's network of ribs, rising from the stained-glass windows, form a curtain characteristic of English Gothic.

TOMB OF AN UNKNOWN NOTABLE. In the Chapel of St. Calixtus in the south arm of the transept is the alabaster tomb shown below. One of the most beautiful pieces of sculpture in Wells Cathedral, it was carved about 1470, but records no longer reveal for certain who was interred here.

somewhat irregular in their plan, showing fantasy in the many columns of rare delicacy and in the colored traceries of the pointed windows. It may be that the retro-choir was intended to serve as a shrine for a saint: unlike other churches of the west of England, Wells Cathedral did not have one to draw pilgrims. There was hope that de Marchia, who was bishop from 1293 to 1302 and whose tomb is in the south transept, might be canonized, but the hope came to naught.

The shape of the Lady Chapel is octagonal; the three western sides open to the retro-choir. The windows have five long perpendicular rows of glass which produce an effect of elongation, then taper off with four, three, two openings and, at the top, only one. The vault is furrowed by ribs leading to a medallion in the center of the ceiling, on which is depicted a bearded Christ. Wells Cathedral was provided with fine cloisters, though it is doubtful that they were intended to serve any actual function. Probably they were intended to imitate the cloisters of monasteries—Wells had no monastic order—simply to add beauty to the imposing ensemble of the church. These cloisters were erected in the middle of the fifteenth century. The windows along the walks, the ribs on the ceilings, the arrangement of the bays have interested scholars. Remains of carvings of scenes of the Passion and of the coats of arms of several bishops are to be seen on the walls.

Inside the cathedral itself, in the north transept, stands a clock dating from the fourteenth century or even earlier. It has the signal distinction of being the oldest in England. It is not known where or by whom it was made; probably at Glastonbury Abbey, where a monk named Peter Lightfoot enjoyed a high reputation as a clockmaker. Complicated works above the face of the clock and behind it transmit power through levers to the figures which make the clock both picturesque and unique. Every hour on the hour, horsemen engage in a tournament. Christ rises and ascends. The symbols of the four Evangelists are carved in low relief at the four corners. Not only are the twenty-four hours of the day and the minutes shown on the clock, but also the days of the month and the phases of the moon. In addition, the Goddess of the Moon, Phoebe, is painted on the central disk of the circular moon window and a Latin inscription proudly states: "This spherical globe shows the world in microcosm, its archetype."

Other unique features of Wells include the Chapter House stairs, reached through the north transept door. The sweep of the steps, built so as to make a right angle turn and continue to the Vicar's Close, is an enchantment. The left side of the steps is worn by the feet which have trodden on them for centuries. Visitors are said to have called these stately steps "the heavenly stairs" from the earliest times. The clustered columns, the bold, narrow vaulting, the traceries on the two oblong and one round window at the end of the stairs have casual irregularity which pleases the imagination. Originally, the stairs ended with a window on the right; this is now the doorway to the Chapter House, built after the stairs were completed. Inside the Chapter House are fifty-one stalls raised above a bench and, on the window ledge, painted on stone, the arms of King James I or James II. The Latin inscription records that he was the "nurturer" of the church: "Jacobus Rex ecclesiae nutritius."

Another original feature of Wells is the stained-glass windows with their strange, abstract arrangements of colors. Still another interesting curiosity of this rich and varied cathedral is its sculpture. Few English churches can boast of their sculpture today: too much havoc was wrought by the Reformation. The façade of Wells is well-nigh unique in its sculptural riches. Chartres, Bourges, Amiens are beyond compare in this respect and the sculpture at Wells cannot claim to such

THE FATHER AND THE SON. One of the rare works of Christian art showing God the Father appears in a detail from the tomb in St. Calixtus Chapel. In this bas-relief the Father, seated in majesty, sustains between His knees a Cross bearing the crucified body of His Son. Not shown is the third member of the Holy Trinity, the Holy Ghost.

A MEDIEVAL ABSTRACT WINDOW. This stained glass window at Wells could almost be a modern painting. It was constructed from pieces of windows destroyed during the Reformation because they represented God in human form and were considered idols. When calm was restored the broken glass was reassembled into the non-representational composition reproduced at the left.

perfection. But it is the finest that an English cathedral offers. Its subjects include floral and fruit decorative motifs, angels, and geometric designs as well as Biblical scenes that are at once concrete and symbolic. In the Resurrection Tier, the dead are shown arising naked from their tombs. Elsewhere the Apostles are arrayed in sets of three, with some carrying the symbols associated with them. The legs of a seated figure are probably all that is left of a "Christ in Majesty." Scenes from the Old Testament are pictured on the south side, scenes from the New Testament on the north. On the central door a central position is given, according to the usual practice of the time, to the Virgin and Child, with angels on each side. The sculpture has been mutilated. It must have been a fine example of deep carving, probably done on the spot as an integral part of the arch.

Inside the cathedral, some fine and famous examples of sculpture are to be seen. On a series of capitals in the north transept the martyrdom of St. Edmund is depicted. The king, crowned but deprived of most of his clothing, is first shot with arrows, then beheaded, and his head is given to a wild beast, which seems either to spurn it or to spare it. On a capital in the south transept is the oft-reproduced carving of a man grimly holding his lower jaw: he is a toothache sufferer. Nearby, on another set of capitals, is carved a humorous record of rustic life. Two men are stealing apples from an orchard. The farmer who owns the property intervenes with a stick and his assistant. One of the thieves escapes with his booty but the farmer's helper is shown on a third capital seizing him by the ear. On the fourth sculpture, he beats the thief mercilessly on the head with a pitchfork.

Outside the cathedral stands the stately Bishop's Palace, with a moat and lodgings for the canons of the chapter. The Vicar's Close, built in the fourteenth century, is connected to the cathedral by a stately chain gate. A cathedral school, one of the oldest educational institutions in England, has existed since the twelfth century.

It is, then, a variety of curious features, some of them unique, that give Wells a conspicuous position among the cathedrals of Britain. The façade is one of the few achievements in England of sculpture and architecture combined. If the great French cathedrals of the early Gothic period—Saint-Denis, Laon, Chartres and the splendidly harmonious shrines of Amiens and Bourges—rank higher in the admiration of art lovers, Wells has an unbroken architectural history which extends from about the beginning of the thirteenth century well into the fourteenth. In its continued development, Wells justifies the claim which has been advanced by Nikolaus Pevsner, in his "Outline of European Architecture": "The architecture of England between 1250 and 1350 was, although the English do not know it, the most forward, the most important and the most inspired in Europe."

THE NAVE OF WELLS. Dear to lovers of English architecture, the nave of Wells Cathedral with its massive pillars and inverted arches has known tumultuous times. In Cromwell's day it was stripped of much of its sumptuous embellishments and a century later it was occupied by troops. But it suffered relatively less damage than other cathedrals and has long been a shrine for those seeking something of old England.

JOYOUS MAGNIFICENCE

BAROQUE
CHURCHES

Few terms in art, ecclesiastical or secular, provoke as much national disagreement as "baroque." For many a decade in some West European languages (English, French, Italian), the idea of baroque was held in suspicion and the use of the word as an adjective was chiefly derogatory. For the Anglo-Saxons, it suggested an art of over-statement, inflated words and over-expressive gestures, as opposed to the reticence dear to English conversation. Palladianism and the Grecian revival were more congenial to Britain, and for a long time to the United States, though hardly to Spanish- and Portuguese-speaking America. The French still feel grave misgivings when they hear foreign critics assert that their classical age was baroque. They stubbornly balk at this description for the Invalides, the Louvre, the Place Vendôme, Versailles, Poussin—even for Le Sueur. Not without some reason they observe that the few French writers who might conceivably be characterized as baroque (Théophile and Tristan L'Hermite) were outlaws or strange rebels in the seventeenth century. For the rest—as Descartes, Corneille, Pascal, Racine, the painters and sculptors of the age of Louis XIV demonstrate—classicism had little difficulty resisting baroque influences introduced by such foreigners as Marino, Bernini or Gongora.

The role of baroque cannot be so easily dispensed with in any consideration of Italian architecture and sculpture after Michelangelo. Still, Jacob Burckhardt, the great Swiss scholar who provided one of the best interpretations of the Italian Renaissance and perhaps the best guide to Italian art, treated baroque as a category only if the term was understood to imply decadence. Benedetto Croce, in a history of the baroque age published in 1929, did not mask his disapproval of what the word connoted. German claims for the baroque as an essential phase of art he would not honor. "Art is never baroque and baroque is never art," he flatly decreed.

To this day, baroque is denounced as bombast, not only by scholars or French nationalist exponents of the classical greatness which corresponded to an age of French hegemony, but also by broadminded apostles of modern Christian art, such as the Dominican Father Couturier. In his private notes, published in March of 1962, Father Couturier declared: "One must side against the baroque. . . . Returning to the baroque is also turning one's back against true life . . . Virtues which are half-naked women, one half for modesty, one for immodesty. The sentimental coquettishness of torsoes, limbs, eyes raised toward heaven, half-opened lips, etc."

Nevertheless, scholars have rehabilitated the word. Our artistic taste has been enriched by a number of gifted critics—Martin Briggs and Geoffrey Scott in England, Corrado Ricci in Italy, Heinrich Wölfflin, Werner Weisbach and others in German-speaking lands—who have enabled us to understand baroque art. A whole artistic era, covering the late sixteenth, much of the seventeenth and part of the eighteenth centuries, has thus been recovered for our enjoyment. Among its many features, the baroque era has one that entitles it to an important section in a portfolio of splendors of Christian art: it attempted to annex, for the benefit of the Christian faith, the wealth made available to European culture by the rediscovery of paganism and by Renaissance humanism.

Critics and exponents of art and culture might have been wise to restrict the use of the term baroque to architecture and the plastic arts, but the concept was applied to poetry and drama, and even stretched to cover prose—that of Rabelais, Cervantes, Bossuet and Sir Thomas Browne. It was applied even more to music, so much so that it is now difficult to think of Vivaldi, Couperin, Scarlatti and Bach apart from the convenient phrase, "baroque music." Walter Pater, who pronounced that "all arts aspire to the condition of music," did not suspect that his aphorism might some day seem truest of the baroque arts, in love with fluidity and "open form" as opposed to "closed form." The result has been a vast amount of glib talk and of loose writing on the subject, with many nationalist prejudices thrown in. For some Germans, baroque is their national mode of expression, and their baroque art makes up for their not having enjoyed a brilliant Renaissance or a harmonious and prosperous classical age. For not a few French scholars, baroque is a Germanic war machine insidiously aimed at upsetting their confidence in French classical achievement; to these French, baroque smacks of irregularity, even of monstrousness, of elephantine ponderousness even when it aims at airy levity—in short, an art that could never have contaminated the subjects of Louis XIII and of Louis XIV, who advocated reason and naturalness as their ideal.

But nationalist prejudices should be banished from the study of art. And at a time when unity is closer to being achieved by Western Europe than at any moment since Charlemagne, they might well be banished from our backward glances at history also. So might much of the pedantry which has lately obscured the specialized writing on the subject of the baroque. Phases (early, full and late baroque) have been distinguished, often arbitrarily and with precision (baseless) in assigning dates. Criteria have been offered which make it easy—far too easy—for any beginner in art history to decide that such a building, such a sculpture or part of a sculpture is, or is not, baroque. Let us leave labels to merchants or, when absolutely necessary, to museum cataloguers. Baroque art addressed itself to the people and endeavored to express their yearning for a renovated Christian faith; it should not become the sole property of pedantic quibblers or of scholars bent on proving that other scholars before them were wrong. Truth, Bacon suggested, may well emerge more easily from error than from confusion. A little common-sense clarity is not out of place in discussing this oft-confused subject.

Indeed, no term designating a style or a mode—classical, romantic, symbolist, surrealist—is ever satisfactory, especially if it is extended from one art to another; from the artistic expression of a mood, inevitably influenced by the unpredictable emergence of genius or of talent, to the history of an age; and from one country to another. This, as noted above, is what has been done with the term baroque, which itself was none too aptly selected from the start. It may well have come from a technical word used in scholastic logic. The word itself had no meaning and therefore long retained a connotation of something slightly absurd. Or it may have been from the Spanish "barrueco" which, in the language of the jewelers, designated something rugged, lacking smoothness and polish. Hence the time it took in several languages to imbue a word originally implying queerness and imperfection with an aura of respectability. Baroque art may be viewed as a Christian reaction against some of the neo-paganism of the Italian Renaissance. It has been presented by some art historians, notably by Werner Weisbach, as specifically the art of the Counter Reformation. It is true that, a few decades after Luther's epoch-making gesture at Wittenberg in 1517, the Roman Catholic Church attempted to steer a more severe course than before: new religious orders were founded, the Inquisition was reinstated, the prolonged Council of Trent (1545-1563) laid down principles for the renovation of Christian art. For a full century after that Council, the Jesuits wielded great power in the Catholic world. Vignola propounded an architectural doctrine in a theoretical work published in 1563. In 1568 he built the Roman church of Gesù, which was to be the model for baroque builders: a single nave, a cupola providing height and light, solemn pillars, a severe appearance in general.

But the Jesuits never imposed one style upon architects. In fact, baroque art flourished best away from Rome and certainly away from Tuscany. It cannot be altogether considered as an outcome of the Counter Reformation, or even as being firmly averse to paganism, for there is sensuousness in Bernini's statues and in the baroque fondness in general for curves and ovals. Italian baroque artists were at least theoretically Catholic, as were the Portuguese and Spanish and a number of the South Germans. But Gryphius and the Silesians in Germany were Protestants—and baroque. The three most celebrated baroque poets of the late sixteenth century in France were Protestants: Du Bartas, D'Aubigné and Jean de Sponde. The Jacobean dramatists in England (Massinger, Webster), the great Milton himself and Otway, who show some baroque influences, were not Catholic. Neither were the Russians, among whom the baroque flourished as if it had sprung from their very soil.

In truth, it is a fruitless endeavor to imprison a varied reality under labels and into periods, just as is any attempt to find uniformity among the countries of Western Europe in a common spirit of the age. In several lands, notably in Italy, the baroque was a reaction against a brilliant Renaissance; it stemmed in part from the desire of the Catholic Church to recapture its hold upon the people and deflect them away from pagan trends in art. In other countries the baroque taste invaded several or almost all of the literary and artistic forms of expression. As Nikolaus Pevsner said: "To these countries the baroque taste came late, but it was taken up with tremendous fervor. Italy has no examples of such orgiastic interpenetration of reality and fiction as can be seen in some few Spanish and many more South German churches of the early eighteenth century."

In France, whatever art may be characterized as specifically baroque cannot be described as a decline from classicism or as a reaction against the Renaissance. Rather, it preceded classicism and was soon merged into it, tamed or (in the eyes of the French) purified by it. Or else it developed with originality only on the frontier regions, hardly fully French as yet, such as Provence (in the sculpture of Pierre Puget), Lorraine (in the etchings of Jacques Callot, the paintings of Georges de La Tour) or the Low Countries (in the work of Philippe de Champaigne of Belgium). It may well be that the existence of a strong middle class in Britain and France, aware of its own power, provided a public which welcomed order, security, meditative art (Poussin, La Tour, Champaigne and Hardouin Mansart in architecture). This public welcomes analysis of the inner man, wisdom, some satirical and burlesque portrayal of manners in literature (the French moralists, Molière, English Restoration comedy, Dryden). Such a public could be entertained only momentarily by the tawdriness of preciosity or by Dionysism blended with religion as was found elsewhere in baroque art. The two countries from which our examples of baroque (or rococo) are taken here, Italy and Germany, both underwent in the sixteenth and seventeenth centuries a breakdown of security which may have induced individuals to search for a refuge in the divine. France, Holland and Britain meanwhile were turning toward science and economic improvement while stressing relations between man and the world rather than those between man and heaven. The Thirty Years' War had laid much of Germany waste and left it uncertain of its future. The sack of Rome in 1527 had struck the Romans like a premonition of divine punishment. In the midst of national humiliation, the churchmen and the artists of those two hopelessly divided countries sought a refuge in saintliness and in heroism. St. Longinus, sculpted by Bernini in St. Peter's, stands as a symbol of the heroic champion of renovated faith. Elsewhere, Bernini and his contemporaries were drawn to the motifs of religious ecstasy and to a mood of quietism—that is, of men's passive submission to the visitations of mystical faith.

Exuberance, willful exaggeration, a stress on what is exceptional and adventurous are found in baroque. In contrast, classicism cherishes a certain restraint, a "Dämpfung" or toning down of what might otherwise stand out too conspicuously as excessive. In baroque one feeling, one impression is selected and inflated, and it is usually the one most likely to arouse surprise. This exaggeration is especially striking because it disdains any submission to what Goethe once praised as the first mark by which a master is recognized, "die Beschränkung," the sense of limitation. The baroque artist gladly leaps beyond conventional or traditional bounds. He favors bigness, even colossality, as Bernini did. And he does not conceal his affection for splendor. He has been portrayed as crashing impetuously into heaven with gold, jewels and bevies of winged cherubs. Extravagance of this order was judged to be appropriate to draw the masses.

In sculpture in particular, dynamic movement, rather than serenity, was the goal of baroque creators. "A man is never as much himself as when he is in motion," said Bernini. Greek sculpture was content with suggesting the potentiality of movement. Baroque sculpture wishes to render motion itself, in progress. The Swiss scholar Heinrich Wöfflin views it as preference for the pictorial over the linear, for the presentation of the interior of a church in depth instead of by parallel planes, with everything leading the eye to the high altar.

In baroque, as a consequence of this preference, mass and color are blended; light and shade are fused into each other; heaven and earth seem to commune. In literature even more than in art, the classical attempt to arrest flux is abandoned; duration is accepted and reveled in. Masks, disguises, and metamorphoses abound on the baroque stage and opera. The world of appearances, denounced as a seductive illusion by Montaigne and by Shakespeare in "Hamlet," is taken to be the one in which art should live and the one it should express.

Illusion, however, should not be taken here to imply deceit; it supplements prosaic reality by transfiguring it into a majestic spectacle rich in symbols. The countries of Western Europe which were least receptive to baroque art, England and France, were also the most persistent opponents of visual illusion and, in the seventeenth and early eighteenth centuries, the most adverse to any form of Christian art. The Puritan revolution in Britain, which closed the stage on which Shakespeare had scored his triumphs, proved equally opposed to anything theatrical in architecture. Palladianism, noble, majestic, often cold, was much more appealing to the English taste.

In the France of Louis XIV—where rebellion had been stifled, dissent silenced, and reason exalted over the capricious instability of the senses—a baroque explosion in literature and the arts would have aroused official distrust. Descartes, Corneille, and Pascal denounced the life of the senses as a perilous triumph of unreason. Poussin, the greatest French painter of his age, spent a great deal of time in Rome, where he could study the Jesuit archetype of baroque churches, the Gesù, and its imitations. He was nevertheless always an advocate of restraint. In his bacchanals and other paintings, Apollonian harmony tones down the Dionysian intoxication to which the figures were in danger of surrendering. He valued above all else the virtue of clarity, which was then the goal of French classicists. He once wrote: "My natural bent forces me to seek well ordered objects, to flee confusion, which is as contrary and hostile to me as light is to darkness."

Only later, near the end of the seventeenth century, did the staid majesty of Versailles begin to pall upon the French and they began, as they periodically do, to feel the temptation of restlessness and sensuous grace. Then the French instilled a pleasant, light note, that of rococo, into the baroque. Louis XIV took matters of taste very seriously and often proved a keener judge than most of his courtiers. He rejected the austere and orderly proposals which his architect, Mansart, brought to him for the castle of La Ménagerie, where the Duchesse de Bourgogne was to live, with the notation: "It appears to me that the subjects are too serious; some youthfulness must be blended with what is to be done here. . . . There must be childhood [de l'enfance] spread everywhere."

Portugal, at one end of the European continent, Russia at the other end, and in the center of Europe, Bavaria, Austria, Czechoslovakia and Switzerland, all were to be the cradles of very diverse forms of baroque architecture. Nüremberg and Würzburg suffered during World War II, but most of the finest examples of that art are still extant. A number of the most striking baroque church and monasteries stood not in cities but in remote villages where their builders seem to have struck a harmony between the structure and the site: Zwiefalten, St. Jakobi surrounded by mountains at Innsbruck, the monastery of Melk on its promontory over the Danube. In the beginnings of what may be termed the baroque era in Central Europe, from 1650 to 1760 or thereabout, Italian models were uppermost in the memories of architects. The church of Gesù inspired St. Michael's in Munich, begun in 1583, and others in Vienna, Innsbruck, Dillingen, Lucerne, Solothurn.

Bavaria and Austria in particular had architects of great renown, the Asam brothers and J. B. Fischer von Erlach, who knew how to express the spirit of their people and their religious aspirations in the baroque churches which they built. The Austrian peasants and mountaineers of Innsbruck and Salzburg, the North Bavarians or Franconians, the West Bavarians or Swabians, are among the most conservative populations of Central Europe. They are respectful of their traditions, devout in their faith and for centuries they were loyal subjects of their sovereigns. Bavarian and Austrian baroque do not display the same showmanship and virtuoso skill as were evinced by Bernini and some of his contemporaries. Catholicism was never endangered in Austria and Bavaria, so it could remain more subdued after the Reformation. Nevertheless, Bavarian and Austrian baroque, and the Swiss as well, united a profusion of ornaments with a deep and moving religious fervor. It is not the fervor of Romanesque art or of the exalted mystical rise of Gothic spires, but it is attuned to the music of Handel and Bach, which to this day makes its richest impact upon us when played in those same baroque churches for which it was composed.

BERNINI AT ST. PETER'S

ROME

The holiest, the hugest and the most impressive church in the Christian world is of course St. Peter's in Rome. To attempt a comprehensive treatment, in pictures or in commentary, would be impossible in a limited space. Here we will concern ourselves only with the breathtaking accomplishments which one seventeenth-century artist achieved in the great basilica which several Popes entrusted to him.

A man of superhuman activity, Giovanni Lorenzo Bernini was almost as multifarious in his talents and almost as gifted as those giants of the Renaissance, Leonardo da Vinci and Michelangelo. Along with Borromini and Pietro da Cortona, he was one of the very great baroque architects in Italy. He was also a sculptor of rare power, a painter and a caricaturist. He had considerable talent as a planner of cities and squares; he designed the most admired fountains in Europe; and he had an organizing and diplomatic skill worthy of a Rubens.

Bernini does not stand with the few supreme creators. But he understood and brilliantly expressed the trends of his age (his lifetime, 1598-1680, almost spanned the seventeenth century) and he molded the face and the spirit of the Eternal City. Descartes, Corneille, Milton, and Rembrandt were Bernini's contemporaries.

A Neapolitan by birth, Bernini was trained in the city of the Popes, where he was taken at the age of eight. Humanism was then at its richest glow. Young Bernini was taught by his father, an artist who originally came from Florence, and he became steeped in Hellenistic tastes. He probably restored or copied ancient statues and was fired with emulation for the tense and burning energy of Michelangelo's late statues. When he was still in his teens he was asked by Scipione Cardinal Borghese to carve four statues. They command our admiration to this day: Aeneas in flight carrying his father, Anchises, in his arms and followed by his son Ascanius; David preparing to aim at Goliath with his sling; Apollo and Daphne, with a bush of laurel actually emerging from the nymph who would escape the god through metamorphosis; and the rape of Persephone by Pluto.

The young artist's versatility, his technical skill, and his mastery of the effects of light on marble, were astonishing. From then on, Bernini was to work for Popes. He organized festivities, multiplying schemes and models for decorations and illuminations for the entertainment of Popes and cardinals. At times he acted like a playboy, at times like a powerful personage. He blended a humanist's refinement with a sincere piety.

The great church that Bernini made greater had a modest beginning. Actually there have been at least three holy edifices on the site, and many artists worked there before Bernini. The site was dictated by an old tradition which held that St. Peter suffered martyrdom between the two outermost "bourns" or boundaries (*inter*

THE PLAZA OF THE POPES. At the majestic square of St. Peter's in Rome, 140 saints in stone have looked down on many centuries of religious drama. At the left is the basilica, the largest in Christendom. To its right are the Vatican buildings, including the Pope's private apartments. (Pages 202-203.)

THE ALTAR OF THE POPES. Over the tomb of St. Peter and under the massive dome created by Michelangelo stands what many consider the ultimate in ecclesiastical baroque, the astonishingly elaborate altar and canopy, or baldaquin, created by Giovanni Bernini. At this altar only the Pope can say Mass.

duas metas) of the Roman emperors' circus on the site of what is now the Vatican. In the center of that circus stood an obelisk nearly eighty feet high, which Caligula had had brought in 37 A.D. from the Temple of the Sun at Heliopolis in Egypt. In 1586 Pope Sixtus V spent a great deal of money and human and mechanical energy to have the obelisk transported away from the church, which had been built alongside it, to the center of St. Peter's square. The tall monolith was afterwards topped with a cross bearing this proud inscription in Latin: "Here is the Cross of the Lord. Flee, His adversaries." A sun dial and a rose of the winds were placed around the pedestal of the obelisk. Two luminous fountains, on the right and left of the obelisk, add their fluid motion and their shade to the splendor of the immense square. Here, in the presence of the most imposing shrine of the Christian religion, and of a monument which has endured more than two thousand years, outlasting many outworn creeds, time and change seem to fade away.

In the earliest centuries of the Christian era, a small oratory marked the spot where St. Peter perished. In the fourth century Emperor Constantine replaced that modest shrine, hardly visible as long as the Christian faith was not openly tolerated, with a sumptuous basilica honoring the Galilean fisherman who was Christ's first delegate in Rome. The basilica was entered through five portals corresponding to its five aisles. (A sixth one, opened only on the occasion of jubilees, was added later.) The façade of Constantine's structure was glitteringly adorned. Mosaics pictured Christ amid figures of the prophets and of His disciples; Constantine himself was depicted there, also praying. A famous symbolic scene, inspired by the fourteenth chapter of St. Matthew, the *navicella*, or vessel of the Church, brought safely through stormy seas under Christ's protection, was later added.

Treasure upon treasure was added to Constantine's basilica: ornaments on the ceiling as well as on the red and green marble of the floor; circles of porphyry on which emperors knelt (as Charlemagne did on Christmas Day of 800) when they went to Rome to be blessed and crowned; medallions, paintings, jewelry. The most ardently worshiped of relics, St. Veronica's veil, or sacred shroud, was preserved there from the twelfth century onward.

The wear and tear of time, barbarian invasions and plundering, and feuds—all combined to endanger the old church. In the middle of the fifteenth century, the great humanist and architect, Leone Battista Alberti, warned Pope Nicholas V that St. Peter's was gravely imperiled by the inadequacy of its foundations on the slope of the Vatican hill. Much audacity was required of both Pope and architect if they were to order the total destruction of a shrine erected by none other than Constantine and under which the remains of St. Peter himself lay. Nicholas

THE CHAIR OF ST. PETER. Behind the high altar of St. Peter's stands the massive chair which Bernini created. Below it are sculpted four Doctors of the Church: Sts. Augustine, Ambrose, John Chrysostom and Athanasius. Above it is a dove surrounded by angels, recalling the promise that the Holy Ghost will be always with the Church. At the sides are the tombs of Pope Urban VIII and Pope Paul III.

and Alberti lacked that audacity but a successor, the impetuous Julius II, did not. In Donato d'Agnolo Bramante, Julius found the destroyer and creator he sought. So in 1505, the old St. Peter's was shattered into ruins. The Romans railed at the Pope's architect, whom they nicknamed "*Maestro Ruinante*—Master of Destruction."

Undaunted, Bramante began to build the new structure. His plan was for a Greek (or square) cross church, with the length of the transept equal to that of the choir and of the nave: it made for greater mathematical simplicity and harmony. The tomb of Julius II, who had not recoiled from the task of erecting a church which was to require whole armies of workmen and fleets of specialists assigned to the upkeep of the building, was to be designed and sculpted by Michelangelo.

After the death of the Pope and Bramante, the design wavered between a church on the Greek plan, as conceived by Bramante and pursued by Antonio da Sangallo, and a Latin cross and rectangular structure as advocated by Raphael. The next artist in charge, Raphael died in 1520 at the age of thirty-seven.

A new Pope, Paul III, elected to the Holy See in 1534, appointed Michelangelo as his adviser and builder. Michelangelo was then working with passionate intensity to add "The Last Judgment" to his Sistine Chapel frescoes. Distracted with sorrow at the death of Vittoria Colonna, to whom he had addressed his most tormented sonnets, and haunted by the approach of death, on which he meditated incessantly, he yet found time to draw plans for a St. Peter's which implied a return to Bramante's Greek cross design, with a gigantic cupola and rows of columns marking the outside wall. Michelangelo's conception is easily visible today for the visitor who walks behind the basilica toward the Vatican. The cupola, reminiscent of Brunelleschi's Florentine cathedral, with its porticoes of double columns, its light buttresses, its miraculous stability in spite of its height (close to four hundred feet) ranks among the great feats of Renaissance architecture in Italy. Michelangelo died in 1564. His great design was fulfilled, and to some extent betrayed, only after his death. Della Porta and Fontana were his successors.

The façade of St. Peter's was the work of Carlo Maderna, who won a competition set up for the design by Pope Paul V. He completed his appointed task by 1614. He has been criticized for the excessive length and height of his front structure, which concealed from view the more stupendous element of the church: Michelangelo's cupola. He did not prove a creative innovator; still, it must be conceded that he maneuvered skillfully around the many obstacles set up by the requirements laid down at St. Peter's by Bramante and Michelangelo.

It was when Maderna died, in 1629, that Bernini became the moving spirit behind the completion of St. Peter's. The present aspect of the great shrine and much of its decoration are the fruits of his talent.

It was a stroke of genius on Bernini's part to imagine and design the circular colonnade leading, in stately and solemn fashion, to the gate of the gigantic edifice. To obtain the room for this spacious conception Bernini had to be ruthless in tearing down houses, even palaces, one of which had been built by Raphael. He wisely eschewed straight lines and right angles. The double circular row of 284 columns and 88 pilasters, surmounted by 140 statues of saints sculpted by Bernini's aides, seems to offer two merciful arms embracing the Christian world. The whole is austere and religious in its geometric order and its Tuscan sobriety, but this classical severity is relieved by the note of fantasy afforded by the arcades and by the variety of the statues.

Athirst for dynamic motion, and endowed with restless vigor, Bernini was even more successful as a sculptor. The work which first strikes the visitor to St. Peter's is an equestrian statue of Constantine on the right in the outer portico. This statue may not rank with the two most celebrated equestrian statues of Italy, at Venice and at Padua, by Verrocchio and Donatello. Nevertheless the tension and momentousness of the scene, the impetuosity of the horse and his rider pushed to victory by a miraculous intervention are admirably suggested.

Inside the basilica, the mind is at first confounded by the vastness of the structure and the heterogeneous variety of styles and of ornaments which would have intimidated an artist less rash and self-assured than Bernini. St. Paul's in London, the cathedrals of Milan and Florence reach only three-fourths of the height of St. Peter's, and the area covered by the Roman edifice is almost three times that of Notre Dame of Paris. Many a visitor has felt oppressed by the vastness, the luxury and the worldliness of St. Peter's. But solitude and inner contemplation can be obtained in many a recess of the immense basilica, and lavishness of ornament is not necessarily, as puritanical Ruskin and positivistic Taine contented, a sign of insincerity in art.

The sumptuousness of the Temple of Solomon as praised in Biblical literature had long haunted the dignitaries of triumphant Christianity before Bernini began his work. And Bernini was true to the spirit of his age, which had already outgrown the austerity of the Counter Reformation and needed to express its faith through an eloquent artistic tribute to God. The nave of St. Peter's he adorned with colored marbles, statues of saints that would be appropriate for a colossal Hercules, and angels perilously close to the figures of Eros that were multiplied in the ancient world during the Hellenistic age. But he should be judged by the baldaquin or canopy, the

MOTHER AND CHILD. A marble statue of a pensive woman tending her child adorns the tomb of Pope Alexander VII. This statue was designed by Bernini when the artist was in his seventies.

Chair of St. Peter, and the mausoleums and statues which he made for the immense basilica. *"È del poeta il fin la meraviglia* — The end and purpose of the poet is to astonish."* This dictum by Giovanni Battista Marino, a contemporary of Bernini, beautifully suits some of Bernini's elaborate endeavors at astonishing his contemporaries. The twisted columns supporting the roof of the canopy and its statues, all topped by the globe and the Cross, were dictated by the model adopted: the twisted pillars of the basilica of Constantine's old St. Peter's, one of which was venerated as a remnant from the Temple of Jerusalem. The huge size of the canopy enabled Bernini to avoid building the traditional baldaquin in stone and rigid columns, which would have impeded the view of the choir and weighed massively on that part of the church. Bernini's purpose, very felicitously reached, was to obtain aerial lightness without sacrificing solidity and dignity, and to preserve the vista of the long basilica. Begun in 1624 on the invitation of Pope Urban VII, the canopy was inaugurated on the feast day of St. Peter in 1633. Only the Pope can celebrate Mass from the papal altar thus built over the grave of the saint.

Much later, between 1657 and 1666, Bernini erected the famous Cathedra, or Throne, of St. Peter in the apse of the church. A relic of wood encrusted with ivory, revered in Constantine's basilica as a fragment of the chair on which the Apostle had sat, was placed in the new Church of St. Peter's by Pope Alexander VII. Bernini provided a structure worthy of the august fragment. He built a pedestal of marble, lavished black bronze and gold on it, hung chubby angels and draperies in clouds above it, and supported the chair itself with four huge bronze statues of Doctors of the Church: St. Ambrose and St. Augustine representing the Latin Church, St. Athanasius and St. John Chrysostom the Greek. That chair, insolently baroque, extravagantly ornate, symbolically expressive, was the assertion of a new spirit that was by then victorious in Italian art. Effects normally reserved for the brush were now being created with the chisel. Space was suggested by a masterful use of light.

Three sculptures represent Bernini at his best. One is a statue of St. Longinus, the Roman centurion, dramatically holding the spear on Calvary. Another is a statue of imperious Urban VII. The third is Urban's mausoleum, on the right side of the apse of St. Peter's. Charity and Justice stand below the pontiff, real and strong matrons surrounded by infants, but rapt in languor. Between them, Death climbs on the sarcophagus, winged, but with the arms and body of a skeleton: he inscribes on a black tablet the name of Urban VIII, whose statue on top of the sarcophagus expresses energy and dignity. It is probably Bernini's masterpiece—but only one of the works that make the Eternal City to a considerable extent the city of Giovanni Lorenzo Bernini.

THE CHURCH OF OUR LADY

ZWIEFALTEN

Man's sensitivity probably reached greater depths in the past, when he was not incessantly distracted by the ease of communications or by the facility with which pictures are reproduced today. The inhabitant of a Greek or of a medieval city, imprisoned in his own circumscribed and unchanging world, hungered for the variety imparted by legends and he lent a ready ear to fanciful or fantastic tales. So, too, modern man seeks entertainment or cultural enrichment in viewing people, edifices and pictures that are different from those which surround him. Hence our interest in some of the strangest art of the seventeenth and eighteenth centuries in Portugal, in Spanish America, and in Central Europe. A munificently decorated and even ostentatious church like that of Zwiefalten may at first jolt the taste that has been nurtured in many of us by admiration of classical Palladian or modern functional architecture. But it presents a challenge to our taste, as it does to the photographer.

Zwiefalten is the only example in this volume of religious art drawn from the two centuries and a half between St. Peter's of Rome and the beginnings of a new church architecture from 1930 onward. This is of course not to say that religion itself suddenly declined in that long interval. Christianity then spread to other worlds (Asia, America, later Africa). In the countries of Western Europe which had long been its cradle it was revivified and deepened. It became even more aware than before of the ideas of social justice, of fraternity, of salvation for all of one's fellow beings as well as for oneself. No period of literature since the Renaissance was more thoroughly permeated with religious and anguished metaphysical yearning than the one which followed the advent of romanticism in several lands. But except in music, very few great works of art were inspired by Christian sensibility. Thousands of churches were erected; statues, paintings were bought in large numbers to adorn them, and often, alas! to banalize and cheapen them. No original style was created. Very little great sculpture emerged throughout the whole of this period.

The sumptuous church of Zwiefalten commands our attention as architecture, sculpture and painting. It invites us, moreover, to give some thought to the vital question of the relationship of an art to the people behind it and to that of a style, the rococo, which has been dimmed by clouds of arguing and pettifogging.

Zwiefalten is situated forty miles south of Stuttgart in southern Germany, a region which was profoundly marked by its nearness to Austria and to Italy. This region remained faithful to Rome after Luther's schism and proved receptive to the Counter Reformation. Much of the art inspired by the Counter Reformation was determinedly didactic. It aimed at instilling again the truths of revealed religion into the faithful. The long central nave in the Latin cross directed the attention and the piety of the congregation toward the high altar. Pictures representing the life and the Passion of the Savior assisted them in their spiritual fervor. The minds were to be persuaded and oriented toward faith, even more than the hearts were to be moved. One of the ablest students of that art, Kurt Heinz, has underlined the differences between that haughty, awe-inspiring art (St. Peter's, Salzburg Cathedral, St. Michael's at Munich), which appears to propose dogmatic truths to the faithful, and the warmer, more familiar atmosphere created in churches like that of Our Lady of Zwiefalten. The latter were more in harmony with a form of popular piety which became widespread in the eighteenth century. For that age of enlightenment and, as is commonly assumed, of disbelief was in effect an age of mysticism and of quietism for the masses of Central Europe, of so-called "Voltairean France," and of England, the home of the Quakers and of John Wesley. Quietism, which advocates a calm, passively receptive attitude to the visitations of the divine in man, spread swiftly in some French ecclesiastical circles, among English Protestants and the German Catholics.

A momentous change occurred in Europe in the late seventeenth and early eighteenth centuries. Religion was no longer necessarily conceived, as Luther, Calvin, Pascal had conceived it, as Kierkegaard did later and as other advocates of *Angst* do today, as inevitably anguished, tragic and entailing a condemnation of a world addicted to sin. The Jesuits on one side, deists, skeptics and epicureans on the other, realized that a new spirit had emerged, with new notions, such as progress, comfort and *bien être*—well being and welfare. They dimly sensed that Christianity might well alienate the modern world altogether if ascetic severity were stressed and emphasis was placed on the Augustinian denial of men's ability to work out their salvation. They came to terms with mundane motives and with human frailty. They drew the heavens nearer to earth, as rococo art does. The sacred and the profane, the divine and the human, married with each other and metamorphosed into one another, exemplify a new view of life, which reoriented the course of Christianity. Curiously enough, that happened at the very moment when the power of the Jesuits themselves had declined in Western Europe and when their order was near being dissolved. (It was dissolved in 1773 but restored in 1814.)

"The idea of a purely didactic ornamentation," writes Kurt Heinz, "had to be given up when the new mystical trend of quietism called for a new form of devout piety. The Greek cross design again became important: its securely closed space, of equal length and breadth, afforded the faithful the calm needed for contemplative piety. Baroque mysticism is characterized both by the piety of the soul which loses itself in the truths of religion

A SUMPTUOUS INTERIOR. Built as the age of the baroque was swirling off into the rococo style, Zwiefalten is a tumbling profusion of celestial personalities and happenings represented in architecture, painting and sculpture. The Saints and the angels swarm over the church's walls and ceilings and the Christ Child sends forth His rays of grace.

(Pages 216-217)

A DEMURE EXTERIOR. Set snugly in the village of Zwiefalten in southern Germany is the Benedictine Abbey of Our Lady. It was built in the eighteenth century, on the site of a monastery dating back to the eleventh century wars of the Guelphs and the Ghibellines. Its exterior offers little hint of the exciting treasures it contains.

and by the exaltation of religious sensibility. Architecture, painting and sculpture must thus provide inspiration to that twofold trend. The members of the congregation are more deeply moved by the atmosphere created than by the message dispensed by the church. The Latin rectangular plan was often abandoned by the church designers of southern Germany for a combination of Greek and Latin crosses. In the Church of Our Lady of Zwiefalten an attempt was made to combine the Greek and the Latin orders, to obey both the traditional liturgical precepts and the requirements of a shrine favorable to serene meditation. Similarly, the ornamentation was designed to satisfy equally the needs for individual worship and for popular piety, which called for separate chapels with their own favorite saints, and the grandiose and all-embracing harmony of the whole, in which the soul might feel lost in the divine.

The Church of Our Lady was built by the Benedictines. It was a quarter century in the building, from 1738 to 1766, but its unity of style survived the span of time. The principal architect, Johann Michael Fischer, born in 1692, had studied in Austria with some of his renowned predecessors there. While less of a innovator than they, he drove the baroque manner to interesting conclusions; today his edifice is considered not so much a climax of the baroque as an independent rococo ensemble. The two terms, and the two styles, cannot be assumed to be altogether equivalent. When he became the actual master of the work at Zwiefalten, Fischer was not free to alter the construction of the choir, which was already far along. He did do away with a cupola which would have interfered with his conception of the interior space and the lighting effects which he had planned. He chose instead a rather low ceiling decorated with frescoes. He also abandoned the project of a nave divided by arches between the entrance and the choir. He sought, instead, through a long oval fresco, to link the several vaults together and produce an impression of unity.

Other devices, such as the galleries of the jube, the side chapels opening on the nave itself, the continuity of the painting and of the statuary—all contribute to the concept of removing any barrier between this world and the supernatural world that is symbolized and suggested. The architect was most happily assisted by a painter, Franz Josef Spiegler, and a sculptor, Johann Michael Feichtmayr. On the ceiling, there is a scene of St. Benedict receiving rays of grace from the Christ Child; this the painter rendered with splendidly orchestrated motion and, at the same time, combined it with the august suspense of a momentous religious event. The dramatic events depicted in the chapels which line the nave are just as harmoniously attuned to the architecture of the church.

AN ANGEL OF THE HIGH ALTAR. At Zwiefalten angels are everywhere, hovering in the air, serving as guards of honor or messengers, or pointing to the sacred events taking place in other statue groups or in the paintings. The sculptured angel shown on the opposite page holds back the stucco drapery around the escutcheon on which the monogram of the Blessed Virgin is written in gold.

Feichtmayr, who was assisted by Joseph Christian, was a sculptor of the first rank. The number of statues which he and Christian erected is prodigious: close to one thousand. They are no more monotonous, no more forced than the creations of a Rubens or of a Delacroix. An angel of extraordinary beauty, perfect features and graceful pose, with the small finger of his right hand poised on his lips as a symbol of the sanctity of Catholic confession, is perhaps the sculptor's most delicate achievement. The angel of the high altar, holding back the draperies which decorate the name of the Virgin, is more coyly aware of his grace and somewhat falsely naïve. Gravely tragic is the angel of Ezekiel's vision, isolated amid lavish decorative motifs, reminding the faithful of the Eternal, to Whom his left hand points. Another angel, more tortuous in his involved shape, takes St. Benedict to heaven. The Negro of the cupola, with expressive, ardent eye, is radiant with picturesque humor; he stands for the dark continent to be evangelized. Elsewhere in the church, a stucco monkey is shown painting a portrait which conveys only the outward beauty of the flesh and none of the spiritual beauty of the model; it amusingly symbolizes false art. The sculpture of Christ on the Cross, above beams radiated by the Holy Spirit, stands among the very few great statues of the Crucifixion done in the last two centuries and a half. The most rococo aspects of this rococo structure are the stalls of the choir, made of glittering walnut and maple, adorned with curves and tendrils, surmounted with involuted and pointed motifs, with a profusion of angels poised on the backs of the benches. There are even some angels perched on the organ pipes.

At Zwiefalten the three arts—architecture, sculpture, painting—merge into one another and borrow the effects of each other in a manner which anticipates the ambitious synthesis of the arts attempted by Wagner much later. The character of the whole is predominantly decorative, with an abundance of white stucco, well fitted for carved figures, which appear to float in the air and to leap into space. The whole is instinct with dynamic motion, as if earth attempted to reach to the skies or if the church itself had become heaven and no boundary stands between earthly matter and men's religious dreams on the one hand and the celestial world on the other. There is something theatrical in that art, an ardent creativeness married to a lavish display of ornaments which has been either praised in rapturous terms by the admirers of that style (most of them, until recently, German or Central European) or disparaged by those who condemn it as "distracting trumpery." An example of the first is afforded by the German art historian A. E. Brinckmann. Lauding the exuberant decoration of churches such as Zwiefalten, he contends that it testifies to "the psychic power of the German soul. . . . The wealth of rococo art is unlimited,

THE ANGEL OF THE VISION. On the opposite page Feichtmayr's sculpture shows the angel who in the vision of Ezekiel warned of the coming of God and the Four Horsemen at the end of the world.   The angel appears to float in mid-air, linking people on earth and in heaven.

THE ANGEL OF BENEDICT. In a church founded by the Benedictines there must be, of course, an altar dedicated to St. Benedict. Atop it, as shown at the right, an angel is preparing to lead the saint to his eternal reward in heaven amid a dazzling golden light that symbolizes the splendors of the celestial mansion.

THE LITTLE BLACK ANGEL. Amid works representing peoples of all parts of the world singing the praises of Mary, queen of all saints, the sculpture at the left seems to have stepped directly from a fresco to send its voice soaring high above all the others.

like the moves of the German spirit. . . . To grasp the whole significance of those spaces, one must have listened to Bach's fugues in that setting... An ecstasy then arises which seizes and carries everything dizzily and exalts the listeners toward God, like specks of dust whirling in eternal light."

Other German writers are more restrained. The sanest and wisest plea for rococo was formulated by Nikolaus Pevsner. He granted its excesses, its stress on declamatory attitudes, its profusion of cherubs and of martyrs; but, he asked, is such an art therefore necessarily insincere? (Emile Mâle had earlier raised a similar question, though referring to Italian and Spanish examples rather than German ones: "The extreme skill of those artists raises doubts as to their sincerity. The attitudes learned from earlier masters, the devices of composition, those angels who populate the sky in order to fill the gaps in a painting, that rhythm of dance of the statues, those draperies agitated by a storm, all that motion fails to satisfy the admirer of the Middle Ages and of their silent fervor." Nevertheless, he said, the rococo artists gave expression to things which had not been expressed by the Middle Ages.) Pevsner argued simply that innumerable souls in Bavaria and elsewhere had found religious comfort and experienced fervor in those churches. Luxurious, even superfluously so in our eyes, they certainly are. But it is touchingly naïve of some religious people to wish to make God's house, as Solomon did his temple, worthy of the Creator and their church a fitting image of the Celestial Jerusalem. It is naïve also to attempt, through stone, wood and stucco, to imitate the motions of angels flying and of saints suffering, but it is not to be condemned outright for that reason. Possevinus, a late sixteenth century Jesuit quoted by Mr. Pevsner, formulated the esthetic reflection underlying much of baroque and rococo art in these words: "The greatest art is to reproduce the thing itself, their torments in the case of the martyrs, their tears in the case of the weeping, their glory in the case of those transported to heaven."

The word "rococo" is a misleading one, even more so than "Romanesque," "Gothic" and "baroque." It seems to have been coined on the analogy of "barocco," as a form of disparagement, at the end of the eighteenth century in France. It came from "rocaille" and alluded to the artificial grottoes which Bernard Palissy had built for the Connétable de Montmorency and which Louis XIV built for the apartments of his mistresses. Stendhal in 1828 used the word with scorn, but Victor Hugo in 1839 and the Goncourts in 1860 used it in a favorable connotation. With the French, rococo is still associated with the notion of shells, scrolls, wreaths of flowers, florid and even tawdry ornaments, quaint china and light, soft, mauve or gilded colors on paintings or frames.

MASTERPIECES IN WALNUT AND MAPLE. The ornate
stalls of the choir, fitted with folding seats, in which generations of
monks have sat and sung praises to God, are carved in intricate curves,
swirls and frolicking angels. Above them gold reliefs on the backs
of the benches depict scenes from the lives of Christ and His Mother.

It usually was limited to the inside decoration of buildings such as the Hotel de Soubise and eighteenth century mansions. It seldom referred to churches.

Historians of taste are overfond of categorizing. It has always proved difficult for them to devise a convenient word to designate the periods which followed the Italian Renaissance, French classicism and the age of Shakespeare or that of Milton in Britain. English labels, referring to sovereigns (Caroline poets, Augustan age, Victorian, Georgian or Edwardian eras), are applicable nowhere else in Europe, and do not go unquestioned in Britain itself. It is too artificial and meaningless to speak of post-classicism and of pre-romanticism, or as some German historians have done, of "romantic classicism" and of *Rokokoklassizismus*. It happens, moreover, that the years when the rococo flourished in Europe in some of the arts, from 1720 or so to 1765, were followed by a recurrence of classical taste, fostered by the discovery of Pompeii and Herculaneum. With the accession of Louis XVI, in France at least, the rococo had spent itself. In England, a Gothic revival had set in and romantic figures appeared, just as they had in Germany with Burger, Herder, and the *Sturm und Drang*.

In France rococo taste in no way stemmed from the baroque. Elsewhere, particularly in Germany, where the rococo may appear to have been the climax of the baroque, the later phase showed none of the dramatic sense, none of the impetuous movement of baroque. It played on the surface of self-contained and independent elements while the forms in baroque sprang from the mass and gave unity to the whole structure.

The modern revival of interest in the rococo has helped us to a better understanding of that most complex of ages, the eighteenth century. Far from being adequately summed up as "the age of reason" or "the era of enlightenment," it was perpetually torn between the desire to believe in, and to bring about, the sovereignty of reason and the longing for the irrational—sentiment and even sentimentality, passion, revolutionary impulses. That age celebrated mundane joys and luxury, nowhere with greater zest than in Voltaire's "Le Mondain" and "Apologie du luxe" or in Watteau's dreams of Cythera. But it dimly realized that in doing so it was only indulging an impossible dream. Nostalgia as well as weariness lurk in Watteau's paintings, in Voltaire's playful epistles, as they do in rococo art. The tragic was banished temporarily and artificially, but it was soon to return triumphant with the end of the century, the Terror and the upheaval of political Europe. Religion was then humanized. Sin was no longer treated as repulsive or as unredeemable, but the romantic revolt was to restore the obsession with the dark world of the unconscious, with the workings of Satan and the problem of evil.

THE GREAT CARVED PULPIT.   A monument in itself, the pulpit is supported from below by the Tree of Knowledge with its fruit, which is death.   Above it are the radiant beams of the Holy Ghost and above them a sculpture of Christ on the Cross presented here not to evoke pity or compassion but as a symbol of the greatness and power of God.   About the crucified figure, some of them embracing it, float the angels.

A RENASCENCE OF SACRED ART

MODERN
CHURCHES

The revival in this century of a bold religious, or sacred, art, as it is called in Europe, stands as one of the most significant developments in modern art and a manifestation of the determined adaptation of religion, especially of the Roman Catholic faith, to contemporary society.

At the end of the nineteenth century, encyclicals deplored, as the greatest scandal of the modern world, the alienation of the masses in Western industrial societies from traditional Christianity. The disciples of Christ and the followers of St. Paul were humble fishermen, carpenters, weavers of tents. But artisans and workmen of the late nineteenth century were not made to feel that Christ's message was addressed to them. Religious sermons and services too often seemed directed to the middle class and the affluent section of society. The concerns of our time and of the common man were hardly heeded. The architecture and the decoration of the churches pursued models set long ago by Byzantine or Gothic builders. No collaboration of the people was requested or welcomed in their designing. A conventional, sugary sweetness prevailed where once scenes of the death of Christ and of the Last Judgment were daring and tragic.

In several lands of the West, especially in Belgium and France, a new spirit moved in shortly before and during World War II. A great Pope, John XXIII, in his encyclical "Pacem in terris" (Easter 1963) and in the testament which he left after he died in June 1963, defined the Church's attitude toward modern industrial societies. He recommended simplicity and poverty to the Church. It mattered but little to Western man if he conquered the world and spread his faith to outlying continents but lost his own soul and the creative inspiration which had always, in thought, spirituality and art, made the West great.

In France, a few independent spirits, great pioneers of the Catholic faith, had denounced the decadence of sacred art in the last century. The most brilliant age of painting since the Renaissance had then dawned in France, encompassing Delacroix, the Impressionists, Van Gogh and Cézanne. Sculpture flourished, soon to create master-pieces even in lands like Britain, which had produced none in the past. Not one of those artists was approached by the Church to help it renovate its decoration. In an era of expansion of science, of new engineering processes devised for new building materials, of original religious thought and, in France at least, of powerful Catholic literature, builders of churches dared not attempt innovations. As early as 1919, Paul Claudel, a former ambassador to the United States and the greatest Catholic poet of modern France, deplored the decay of sacred art as a result of "the divorce between the propositions of the Faith and the powers of imagination and of sensibility, which are eminently the powers of the artist." He added with sad vehemence: "To him who dares to look at them, modern churches have the pathetic interest of a confession laden with meaning. Their ugliness is the extension on the outside of all our faults: indigent weakness and timidity of faith and of feeling, dryness of heart, disgust with the supernatural, exaggeration of individual and disorderly practice, worldly luxury, avariciousness, boastfulness, sullenness, pharisaism, bombast."

Jacques Maritain, the chief neo-scholastic philosopher of our time and the friend of many artists, had advised them in 1927 in "Art and Scholasticism": "Be Christian and try to do a beautiful work in which your heart will express itself. Do not attempt to 'do something Christian'." He stated his view concisely: "Christian art is the art of man redeemed." Marie-Alain Couturier, to whom a great deal of the splendid French achievement in sacred art must be credited, was fond of quoting Delacroix's noble motto: "One must always wager in favor of genius." He added: "Great things must be entrusted to great men." Father Couturier fought against the esthetics that had been inherited from the late Italian Renaissance (Guido Reni), from Murillo in Spain and from the so-called Jesuit style in the eighteenth century, which mistook gentleness and set smiles in religious art for authentic Christianity: this at a time when Rembrandt, Vermeer, Velásquez, Caravaggio and Goya were alive and could have been called upon to work for churches.

Today members of the Jewish faith (Chagall, Lipchitz) and agnostic artists (Le Corbusier, Matisse, Léger, Bonnard, Germaine Richier) have plunged deeper into the vital sources of religious artistic inspiration than those of Catholic belief. Their testimony and their achievement enhanced the faith and drew truly religious souls to Assy, Coventry, Ronchamp and Vence. They opened up vistas on the infinite, whatever their own convictions were. Pius XII, the predecessor of John XXIII at the Papal See, once defined their mission in an address to artists: "The function of all art is to break the constricting and anguishing circle of the finite in which man is encompassed as long as he lives in this world, and to open a window to his mind which yearns for the infinite."

The Dominican fathers, who have stood at the vanguard of the Church's contemporary revival of interest in sacred art, have had to defend it, even at its noblest, against conventionalism and timorousness. One of them, Pius-Raymond Régamey, published a book defending their position. He set these conditions for the acceptance of such art by Christians: that the works be didactic and symbolic, as Christian art was from the earliest centuries of the new faith; that it further contemplation in the onlookers, deepen their feeling for the divine and glorify the Redeemer. Artists who created art that could do these things owed no accounting of their inspiration to any authority. Their art should be born of a feeling of necessity. Matisse, one of those artists who was commissioned to decorate a chapel by Father Couturier, was questioned whether an artist who professes no religion could do a work of sacred art. The answer Matisse gave was direct. He replied: "Look at the completed work. Does it invite the viewer to serene meditation and to peace? That is the question."

Manessier, perhaps the greatest Catholic painter in France since Rouault's death, explained his conception of that art, which he made bold and ardent, in these somber words which few observers of contemporary life could dispute: "Today an essentially tragic era makes the condition of man tragic. We would not offer our own message worthily if we did not accept also the necessity of being tragic, and being so in our art.

But we realize that the tragedy of man may well coincide with divine peace, thanks to the Christian practice of inner life. In such a living union the whole meaning of a virile Christian art resides today."

Modern religious architecture has aroused less furious controversies than the sculptural or pictorial portrayals (many would say "distortions") of Christ on His Cross, of the Virgin and Child, of St. John the Baptist or of the Crown of Thorns. The reason is obvious. Modern architecture, stressing bareness, simplicity, functionalism, eschewing luxury and a sweetness which might easily become insipid, broke with habit less flagrantly. It seemed attuned to a Christianity which wanted to cease being the monopoly of the rich and the possessors and to reach out to the underprivileged or rebellious in our midst, whom Communism was attracting.

In 1922, Auguste Perret erected an unassuming church in concrete, severe but in harmony with the poor suburb of Paris where it stood, Raincy. The Swiss followed that example with more audacity. Karl Moser completed St. Anthony's at Basel in 1929, with marked purity in the design and the walls almost wholly replaced by glass. A disciple of Moser, Fritz Metzger, achieved an even more elegant church, St. Charles', in Lucerne. At Basel again, Hermann Baur reached effects of majesty through extreme simplicity.

A master of religious architecture in all its boldness—in the writer's opinion, the master—is Swiss-born Le Corbusier. His chapel at Ronchamp, in France, near Basel, ranks among the truly great works of the modern age. It stands in harmony with the site of the Vosges and the valley below. It receives light from skillfully disposed apertures. Its shape is singular but strikes many an onlooker as the only one which could have fitted the site and the religious feelings which the church fosters. Foolishly, the detractors of Le Corbusier attempted to dismiss his work as baroque, a word which, in French at any rate, long had unfavorable connotations. "I hate the term [baroque]," the architect has declared with vehemence, "and never have liked or looked at, or been able to admit baroque art... Abstract art is the 'raison d'être' of Ronchamp, the language of architecture... the compass needle pointing to that space which is beyond description."

The chapel at Ronchamp was dedicated in 1955 by the Bishop of Besançon. At the same time, having been invited by the Lyons chapter of the Dominicans, Le Corbusier set to work on a church with cloister, library, refectory and other parts of their monastery, Sainte-Marie de la Tourette, at Eveux near Lyons. On October 19, 1960, Cardinal Gerlier, Archbishop of Lyons, at the dedication of the new edifice, retracted his earlier objections to modern architecture for Christian buildings. The cardinal dedicated the marvelous ensemble, and in doing so he praised the architect who, without sharing the faith of those who were to live and pray in it, but respecting it, had created "a great achievement for the Church."

Sacred architecture of the years 1940-64 is perhaps most famous for two handsome and original structures in a contemporary style and built with modern techniques which are treated in the following pages: the Church of Assy, in the mountains of Savoy near Mont Blanc, and the Cathedral of Coventry in England. But it has also inspired very original synagogues and a few bold Christian churches in the United States.

Assy and Coventry, among other holy edifices, make it possible to say that men and women of the second half of the twentieth century, threatened by atomic pulverization as those of the Middle Ages thought themselves threatened by the end of the earthly world, have responded to the challenge with conviction and with some beauty.

OUR LADY OF ALL GRACE

PLATEAU D'ASSY

Assy, the birthplace of much modern religious art, is a small mountain village near the Arve river in Haute-Savoie. Its altitude is over three thousand feet. It faces south, looking at Mont Blanc. Since 1926 a number of sanatoriums for consumptives have been established there, and soon a church proved necessary for the growing community of invalids and caretakers, nurses, hotel keepers, and farmers. A Dominican priest, Father Devémy, canon of a nearby village, was entrusted with the construction. He commissioned an architect of the region, Maurice Novarina, to erect a simple and modest church, in green granite and grey marble, that could withstand the heavy winter snowfalls. It has a square campanile on the right, also effectively simple, ending in an angular shape and surmounted by a cross. Eight short pillars support the pointed roof. The whole is unassuming and intelligently functional and deserves praise as such.

But the church at Assy is best known for its decoration. Furious controversies have been waged over it, as Catholics took sides for and against some of the works which well known artists executed for it. Objections were made not only against individual works, notably the Christ by Germaine Richier, but also against the result as a whole: the church was said to resemble a museum more than it did a shrine for worship. However, the varied authorship of the outstanding works at Assy, and their divergencies, both in inspiration and in style, do not detract from the total religious effect of the church. They are all of one age, whereas in the buildings of the past ages, new styles and manners were often superimposed over many years upon the original. In his important volume, "Sacred Art in the Twentieth Century," Father Régamey rightly calls Assy "one of the very few sanctuaries of our time in which we are seized by the *sacred* character of the place just as we are in the most gripping churches of the Middle Ages."

In planning the decoration of his church Canon Devémy received the assistance of a fellow Dominican, Father Marie-Alain Couturier, who was himself a former painter and a friend of many artists and art critics. Father Couturier's writings, which were published for the most part after his death in 1954, are marked by humility and fervor, and are replete with provocative statements on the reintegration of beauty into modern religious architecture. Canon Devémy first went to see Georges Rouault, whose stained glass windows, exhibited in 1939 at the Paris Petit-Palais, had impressed him. The great Catholic painter of modern France agreed to design a number of windows; his designs were skillfully carried out by Paul Bony. Paul Bony also designed other stained glass windows and Couturier himself did windows of St. Theresa of L'Enfant Jésus and St. Raphael in the nave.

GREATNESS IN ART. For the Church of Our Lady of All Grace at Assy, in the French Alps, a number of major modern artists created major works. Constructed of local stone, the church is shown in this photograph as it radiates its brilliance in the dusk.

During World War II, Canon Devémy went to see the great colorist Pierre Bonnard. Bonnard, who was approaching eighty, was then vacationing in the Assy region. The priest has himself recorded the story of that meeting: "Come in," said the painter. "You have well chosen your day. I have just this morning buried my wife." Canon Devémy was never so embarrassed in his life. But Bonnard brushed aside his profuse apologies and continued: "It gives me pleasure to see you . . . . One cannot weep all the time . . . ." He took his visitor into his modest dining room, furnished in the "petit bourgeois" manner: in the middle of the room was a long table with a dish of fruit; on the walls hung two Renoirs.

Devémy explained his plans for his church and said how marvelous he thought it would be to have a St. François de Sales painted by Bonnard. The artist was surprised when told that Rouault had already done a stained glass window. Bonnard agreed to accept the commission and asked for documents on St. François, the seventeenth century saint from Savoy who ranks among the finest prose writers of his age. Bonnard did the painting. When Devémy tried to thank him he replied: "The thanks should come from me. I am grateful to you to have allowed me to paint that picture which interested me greatly and taught me so much about my métier."

The front of the church was entrusted to Fernand Léger, to be decorated with mosaics. To him is due the credit for the richly colored, joyful picture of the Virgin, Our Lady of All Grace, welcoming the sick and the convalescents of the sanatoriums around Assy. Invocations from the Litanies to the Virgin—"Sealed Fountain," "Mystical Rose," "Morning Star," "Closed Garden," "Tower of Ivory," etc.—are elegantly inscribed on the two sides of the central mosaic. The front has more order and neatness than fantasy and warmth, as is usual in the works of Léger, that robust successor to Cubism.

Inside, the tapestry which was conceived by Lurçat for the wall over the choir displays greater boldness. It was manufactured at Aubusson and ranks among the finest achievements by this great reviver of the art of tapestry in our time. It is composed with rigor, inside a vast rectangle, and it is vibrant with life and fantasy. Two vertical rectangles on the sides frame the inner rectangles. Black and white stand in contrast in the play of colors, to suggest the struggle between light and darkness, good and evil. As in many a medieval tapestry, like the very great one at Angers, the theme and the inspiration are derived from the Book of Revelation in the New Testament (XII, 1-10). A woman, "clad in the sun," the moon under her feet, and with twelve stars around her head, faces the dragon which threatens to devour her baby soon to be born. (The same scene is

239

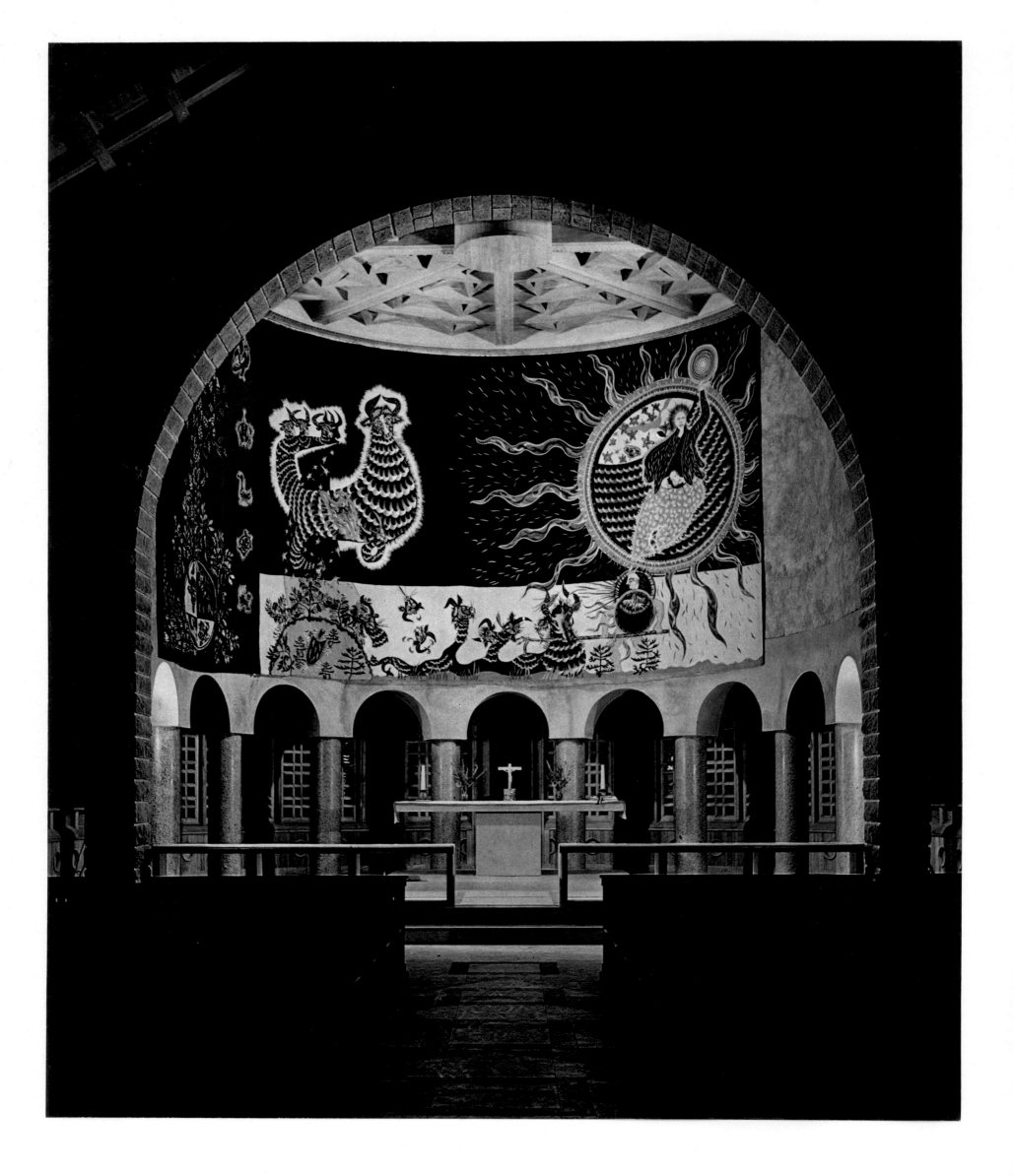

THE MANY MARVELS OF ST. JOHN. The tapestry behind the altar at Assy, designed by Jean Lurçat, draws its inspiration from the Revelation of St. John. At the right is the woman "clad in the sun," at the left the dragon of "seven heads and ten horns" waiting to eat her unborn son. Below them is Archangel Michael fighting the dragon. The panel at the far left represents the creation of the world; the one at right is unseen in this photograph.

illustrated in a painting at St. Savin, shown on page 127.) St. Michael vanquishes the dragon (snake or Satan) and Christ's reign will be assured. The symbolic woman is taken to stand for the Church, incessantly giving birth to Christ, or, according to another interpretation, for the Virgin Mary, mother of God. On the right stands the Tree of Jesse from whose roots a flower will grow. It designates, according to the opening of St. Matthew's gospel, the genealogy of the Savior.

The central position over the altar was originally reserved for a startling and tragic Crucifixion by Germaine Richier. Her sculpture in bronze—rough, stark, and, on first sight, distorted—raised an outcry. It was denounced as being too realistic. The ecclesiastical authorities bowed for a brief while to the clamor of timorous souls and withdrew that eloquent Christ from the church. At the request of many of the faithful, including same of the least sophisticated among them, mountaineers and peasants, who might be considered to have no feeling for the "distorted", it has since been reinstated. It now hangs in the chapel on the left side.

The Crucifixion of Assy is in fact abstract rather than realistic. In the years 1940-45, abstract art had not yet won the recognition which it has since received—a recognition which caused too many to jump on the bandwagon and to practice the technique of abstract art with nothing but facile skill. Back in the forties, conservative opinion branded any abstract work as a departure from the past. But in truth Germaine Richier stood in a time-honored tradition. From the earliest times, artists have distorted reality in order to reach a greater truth. After the invention of photography, sculptors and painters, reacting against the nineteenth century Victorian taste which clamored for reassuring likenesses in art, eschewed the imitation of objects. Vincent van Gogh, in one of his letters to his brother Théo, pathetically remarked, à propos of the lack of appreciation of his art by the public: "My chief desire is to learn how to achieve such inexactness, such anomalies, such changes from reality that there may emerge lies, if one wants to call them that, but lies truer than literal truth." Later, another Dutch painter, Mondrian, an austere Calvinist, forsook imitating reality, as he had done earlier in his career, in order to paint squares, right angles and to achieve a serene equilibrium of shapes. He declared: "When the artist does not represent objects, more room is left for the divine."

Germaine Richier's early sculpture has been compared to nothing less than Donatello's St. John the Baptist in the Bargello in Florence. Her vision of the world was essentially a tragic one, as is that of many a modern creator who is unwilling to follow traditions slavishly but is anxious to express the tormented soul of

WINDOW FOR AN ORGANIST. The organ loft at
Assy is lighted by three windows on musical themes,
designed by Jean Bazaine. The one above depicts St.
Gregory the Great, who established the plain chant used in
Catholic services. The others are of Cecilia, patron of musi-
cians, and of David, who sang his Psalms to his own harp.

modern man. There was nothing but humility and anguish in her sculptures of birds and other animals, or in her rendering of violently disrupting cosmic forces of nature, such as hurricanes.

In her later life, when Germaine Richier was suffering from the cancer which carried her away in 1959, her work became even more stark. Her "Crucifixion" at Assy is considered one of the very few modern treatments of that tragic theme, so forcefully rendered by so many artists in earlier times, which is worthy of the subject. One critic describes it thus: "With her massings of flesh, torn tissues and straining muscles, more piteous even than the dead Christs of the Middle Ages, the artist expresses what every man should find moving: the endless suffering of mankind." Indeed, that sculpture, which may well open a wholly new era in the plastic representation of the Crucifixion, while tragic and powerful, exudes tenderness and moves us to mournful compassion. In the words of Father Régamey, if the viewer "refuses to let himself be hardened by a superficial first impression and remains open to the radiating message of that Christ, . . . he will be forced to admit that here resides one of the strongest suggestions ever successfully offered to us of the mystery contemplated by faith and impossible to represent fully through plastic means."

Elsewhere in the church at Assy are works by three of the greatest artists of the time—Henri Matisse, Georges Braque and Marc Chagall—and a great sculptor, Jacques Lipchitz. Matisse contributed a bright ceramic on the left side altar which depicts St. Dominic as the bearer of the Evangel. Braque is the creator of the gate of the tabernacle, the symbol of which, as in the catacombs and in early Christian monuments, is a fish, since that word in Greek included the initials of the five words designating "Jesus Christ, Son of God, Savior." A powerful bronze sculpture by the Jewish artist Jacques Lipchitz helped make Assy the mecca of modern art that it is. Another Jewish artist, Chagall, composed for the Baptistery Chapel the epic mosaic of the Hebrews led by Moses across the Red Sea. There is a sweeping motion in the scene. Also, under the arm of the angel, Chagall has depicted himself, as a little man with a cane, the symbol of the Wandering Jew.

"A work of art, in order to be religious, should be accomplished religiously, . . . that is, with humility, respect for objects, the sense of mystery in them, in a word, the sense of the presence of God, their creator, in them." These are the words of Father Couturier, and such was the spirit in which a great range of creative artists—including city artists and artisans from the mountains, agnostics, Jews and Catholics—collaborated in the church at Assy in bringing about a renaissance of religious art. Their work is being continued and added to today.

LIGHT FOR THE CHAPEL OF THE DEAD. The stained glass window at Assy dedicated to Saint Veronica is considered the finest of five that Georges Rouault designed and Paul Bony executed for the church. It is located in the Chapel of the Dead at the left side of the entrance. The other creations of the Rouault-Bony collaboration depict scenes from the Passion and from the Book of Isaiah.

CATHEDRAL OF ST. MICHAEL

COVENTRY

When the cathedral at Coventry was redesigned and rebuilt after its destruction in World War II, controversy raged just as furiously in Britain as it had in France over Assy. Three Anglican cathedrals had previously been erected in England in the twentieth century, at Truro, Liverpool and Guildford. None of them had dared to be resolutely of its own age; each was planned in a surviving form of a defunct Gothic style.

The design of Sir Basil Spence for Coventry was selected by three eminent British architects over hundreds of others on August 15, 1951. Queen Elizabeth II laid the foundation stone and later, in May 1962, she attended the consecration of the edifice. Meanwhile the architect had received close to a thousand letters about his design: "eighty per cent of them were rude—the rest very rude." He never wavered. He knew that he had to do in 1960 what the architects of the Gothic cathedrals had done in their own time: to be relevant and meaningful for his day; to utilize the resources of contemporary materials and craftsmanship; not to pay reverence to a tradition that had become effete, but to create a new tradition. "If we cannot express our Christian faith in terms of our time, we might as well pack up," he declared bluntly. The Bishop of Coventry, who had admired Sir Basil's design for the new cathedral from the start, remarked that ninety per cent of the people who had bitterly condemned the plans changed their minds when they saw the completed building. Many visitors to Coventry nowadays find their stay a powerful religious, social and esthetic experience.

The first Coventry cathedral was built in 1053 as the minster for a Benedictine priory. A second was rebuilt in the Gothic manner. A third, in the English Perpendicular style, replaced it early in the fifteenth century. It stood in the middle of a city once famous for its wool trade, for its cloth industry and the prosperous merchant community which lived there. Medieval Coventry's tradesmen were organised into guilds, many of which had their own chapels in St. Michael's: the Grocers, the Dyers, the Cappers and others. The Cappers' Guild, incidentally, still has a room in the cathedral. Known as the Cappers' Room, it is situated among the ruins of the old cathedral. Though most of the ruins were left as they were at the end of the war, the Cappers' meeting place was put back into usable condition. Coventry continued to prosper after medieval times, and many new industries were added to its traditional ones. Among these were leather, glass and watchmaking. In modern times, it became a prominent center for the manufacture of automobiles and aircraft. In 1918, the year World War I ended, Coventry, with its rapidly growing population, was again made the seat of its own diocese, a position it had once held in ancient times but lost in the sixteenth century.

ST. MICHAEL AT COVENTRY. The patron saint of Coventry's cathedral, St. Michael the Archangel, as rendered in a monumental bronze by Sir Jacob Epstein, spreads his wings over the demon at his feet. He looks toward the ruins of the old Coventry cathedral which was destroyed by the demon in men.

Early in World War II, on November 14, 1940, a clear moonlit night, the German Air Force sent wave after wave of bombers to spread incendiary bombs over Coventry. The roof, the walls, the pillars, and the chapels of the cathedral were soon ablaze. The city was razed. Very little remained standing when King George VI came to visit the ruins two days later. Only the spire had survived the devastating attack. It was vowed that the cathedral would rise again. When the time came to rebuild, a spirit of forgiveness had replaced the bitterness of the war of 1939-45. Young Germans came to work on the new church. Other European countries sent gifts and art. On the wall of the destroyed sanctuary these words from St. Paul's Epistle to the Romans were inscribed: "FATHER, FORGIVE. All have sinned, and come short of the glory of God." What remained of the burned-out church was for the most part preserved as it stood: the new cathedral (which faces north, not east) was built to the north of the old, and one approaches it through the battered ruins. The delicate problem of linking the new edifice and the ruins was ingeniously solved with a vast porch and a flight of steps on the east.

The novelty of Sir Basil Spence's plan consisted in the prolific use of steel, glass and of reinforced concrete for the walls; in making the design of the projected cathedral relevant to the everyday interests of the inhabitants of a reborn and active industrial city; and in the avoidance of all that would have been mere imitation of the past—that is, sham. The architect was also anxious to make ample room for the arts in the new building. As at Assy, this aim has its drawbacks, notably in a lack of unity in the total effect. All is not to be equally admired at Coventry. But the total achievement is magnificent.

In the interior, glass decoration makes light and shade play with glittering splendor. The effect is further enhanced by the long, ascending windows reaching to the ceiling. The pillars, in concrete, are slimmer than stone columns could have been, and far more solid. There are no partition walls, there is no jube. Everything is intended to direct the eyes to the altar and to the tapestry above it.

The tapestry, representing Christ in Glory, is by the English painter Graham Sutherland. It has been criticized for its color and its rather stiff design. The figure of Christ is perhaps overpoweringly huge. Beneath Him and between His feet is the figure of a tiny man. Much more praise has been bestowed upon the splendid Baptistery window. The window, which was designed by John Piper, is made of nearly two hundred panes of glass. It symbolizes the Divine Light illuminating the world, and all the colors seem to be fused in its harmony. A huge, rough, handsome boulder, sent from Bethlehem by the Jordanian Government, serves as the font. On

INTO THE NAVE. The passage into the nave of the Coventry cathedral goes through a huge wall of glass. It is composed of ninety panels, many of them engraved with translucent figures of saints and angels designed by John Hutton. Also visible through the glass is the tapestry of Christ in Glory that completely covers the apse.

the left side as the visitor enters, the floor of the Chapel of Unity is a masterly work in mosaic by the Swedish artist Einar Forseth. The stained glass was offered by German churches and presented to Coventry in 1958 by the President of the German Republic. In this chapel is inscribed a phrase from St. John (XVII, 21): "That they all may be one." Other gifts for this unique new-old building came from all over the world. From Stalingrad in officially godless Russia, itself the scene of some of the most savage fighting during the war, came an old ikon. From Tanganyika came a crucifix carved in ebony by an eighteen-year-old boy. From Hong Kong vestments, and from Canada a gift of more than twenty-five thousand dollars. There was a piece of a font from a church in Kweilin which had been destroyed by Japanese bombers, and from Queen Mary came the Bible she had been given for her wedding. To the right of the main altar is the most moving chapel of the whole building: it is meant for private prayer by persons in sorrow who wish to pray to the Lord as He prayed at Gethsemane when His anguish unto death was like a cup to be drained to the dregs. It is called the Chapel of Christ in Gethsemane. The angel who appeared to strengthen Christ is here depicted. At the entrance of the chapel is a screen shaped like a Crown of Thorns, designed by the architect of the building.

At regular intervals on the inside walls of the cathedral artistic tablets, very tastefully disposed, bear sayings from the Gospels. Outside, on the east entrance to the porch of the Cathedral, stands a bold, tall statue, by Sir Jacob Epstein, of the Archangel St. Michael vanquishing the Devil. Compassion rather than exultation in his triumph can be read in the features of the Archangel, whose wings are outspread in a splendid upward thrust. The position of this statue against the wall is as striking as the statue itself.

The cathedral of Coventry is one of the very few modern religious buildings in which the reflection of today's industrial civilization is everywhere present. Pope Pius X once declared: "I want my people to pray over beauty." Religion, in a century which has endured two world wars and after each one has staged a magnificently courageous renaissance, stubbornly refuses to be merely an ornamental adjunct of the lives of the people. It seeks to appeal to the laboring world, to be at the service of the working classes. In Coventry, the builders of a cathedral which stands in the center of an industrial city resorted to the good will and to the skill of the workers who were to pray in the new structure. The Jaguar automobile works, located nearby, provided parts to build the pillars supporting the Chapel of Christ the Servant. The huge crown of thorns around a cross was cast by other workmen of the city; the chapel in which it stands is for the use of the chaplains of industry. The

OLD PRAYERS, MODERN SETTINGS.   The choir stalls and Graham Sutherland's tapestry are modern in design and materials.   The tapestry shows Christ in Glory surrounded by symbols representing the four Evangelists.   Between Christ's feet is the figure of a man, life-sized, but puny before God.

THE CHAPEL OF GETHSEMANE. Designed as a quiet place for those who must pray in torment as did Christ on the eve of His Passion, this chapel is framed in a wrought-iron Crown of Thorns by Sir Basil Spence. Steven Sykes did the fresco of the angel who helped Christ through His bitter hours.

THE NEW, THE OLD. Through the glass partition separating the nave from the porch of the new cathedral can be seen the walls of the old cathedral, destroyed in the bomb attack of 1940. The old walls testify that a church destroyed is the cradle of a new church.

Chapel of Unity, a symbol of tolerance in a country most of whose citizens are divided among several Christian faiths, was designed in the shape of a star: it thus points the ways which lead to Christ. The equipment which serves to retransmit the religious services is likewise modern. Coventry is the first church in the world to have permanent radio and television equipment. The studio is in the crypt and the cameras and microphones are discreetly hidden in the nave, where they are quite unobtrusive.

That vast and functional building is also laden with emotion. The first gesture of the inhabitants of the ravaged city during the war had been to set up two half-burned rafters amid the ruins in the shape of a cross. With nails recovered from the charred remnants, another cross was made which stands today on the high altar. As soon as World War II ended, replicas of the Nail Cross were sent to other cities which had suffered martyrdom— including those of the former enemy and an old ally: Berlin, Hamburg, Volgograd (originally Stalingrad). Symbolic offerings were at once returned to Coventry. The spirit of reconciliation and of Christian fraternity which bids men to look away from the horrors of a destructive war and face a better future is symbolized by several details of the new cathedral and expressed in eight large stone panels, each with an inscription from the Bible.

The cathedral of Coventry has given the British people the proof that they can stand at the vanguard of any artistic movement today without betraying their traditions. The Provost of the reborn church, the Reverend H. C. N. Williams, after enduring the paralyzing objections of those who repeat, "We have never done this before," declared that the modern and artistic building which Coventry built was helping the church to fulfill its function in modern life: to express wholeness in a broken world, to be a coherent society within an incoherent community.

It is worth recalling the words of the Bishop of Coventry himself. The Right Reverend C. K. N. Bardsley is the first Bishop of the Church of England who has witnessed both the consecration and actual completion of his cathedral. "So often," he has said, "one has thought of the Church in terms of Victorian Gothic, and all that went with it, and here [is] something . . . breaking loose from all that and attempting to express the faith in modern terms. The first thing I discovered on coming here was that it wasn't just a great building which was modern but that all those who were associated with it were very modern in their outlook, and were attempting to make the cathedral the center of the whole life of the community."

The center of the whole life of the community! That was what the creators of many ancient great buildings had in mind when they, too, set out to build in their own time.

254

APPENDIX

Sancta Sophia, Istanbul

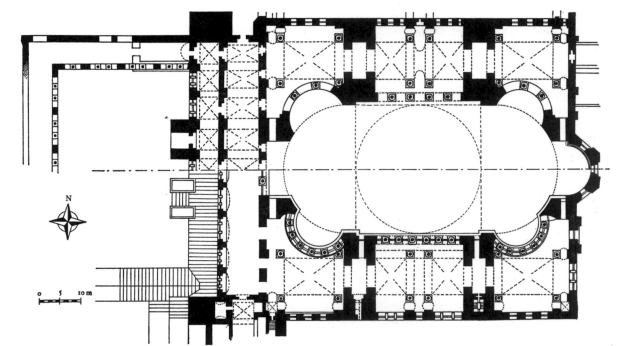

Total length, interior	252 ft.	7 $^2/_3$ in.
Total width, interior	232 ft.	11 $^1/_4$ in.
Width of the central nave.	114 ft.	10 in.
Diameter of the cupola	101 ft.	8 $^1/_2$ in.
Height of the cupola at wallside	183 ft.	8 $^3/_4$ in.

San Vitale, Ravenna

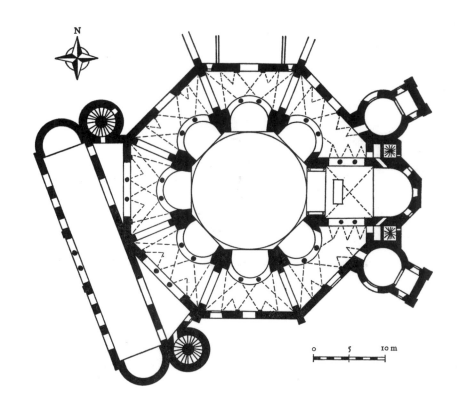

Maximum width	113 ft.	10 $^1/_8$ in.
Length of one side of the octagon	42 ft.	7 $^2/_3$ in.
Width of the atrium	121 ft.	4 $^2/_3$ in.
Diameter of the cupola	54 ft.	1 $^3/_5$ in.
Length of the choir	51 ft.	2 $^1/_6$ in.

St. Mark's, Venice

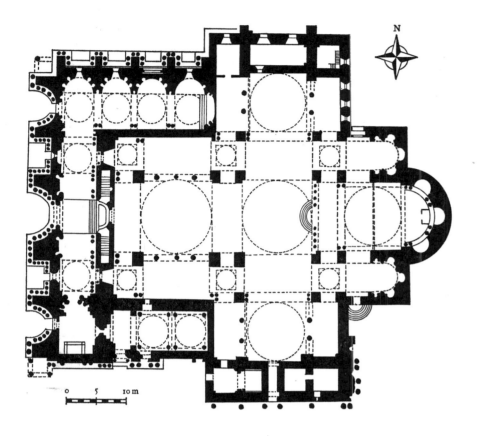

Total length from the central portal to the end of the apse	260 ft.	9 $\frac{9}{10}$ in
Total width of the nave	172 ft.	2 $\frac{9}{10}$ in
Width of the central nave alone	68 ft.	10 $\frac{3}{4}$ in.
Length of the transept	206 ft.	4 $\frac{2}{5}$ in.
Width of transept arm	77 ft.	1 $\frac{1}{5}$ in.
Diameter of the large cupolas	41 ft.	8 in.
Diameter of the cupolas in the transept arms	32 ft.	1 $\frac{4}{5}$ in.
Diameter of the eight small cupolas	19 ft.	3 $\frac{1}{2}$ in.
Height of the cupola in center of transept at wallside	93 ft.	6 in.
Height of the façade	72 ft.	8 in.

St. Magdalen, Vézelay

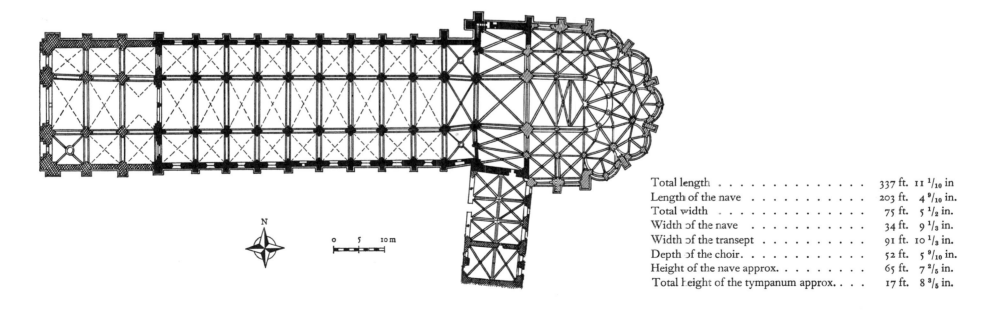

Total length	337 ft.	11 $\frac{1}{10}$ in
Length of the nave	203 ft.	4 $\frac{9}{10}$ in.
Total width	75 ft.	5 $\frac{1}{2}$ in.
Width of the nave	34 ft.	9 $\frac{1}{3}$ in.
Width of the transept	91 ft.	10 $\frac{1}{3}$ in.
Depth of the choir.	52 ft.	5 $\frac{5}{10}$ in.
Height of the nave approx.	65 ft.	7 $\frac{2}{5}$ in.
Total height of the tympanum approx. . . .	17 ft.	8 $\frac{3}{5}$ in.

Minster of Our Lady, Ulm

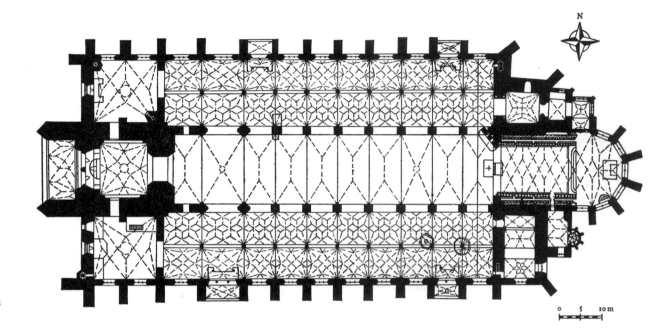

Length of the interior	406 ft. 9 ³/₅ in.
Width	160 ft. 9 ¹/₈ in.
Height of the nave	137 ft. 9 ¹/₂ in.
Height of the tower	528 ft. 2 ¹/₂ in.
Height of the porch	49 ft. 2 ¹/₂ in.
Capacity	27,000 persons

St. Andrew's, Wells

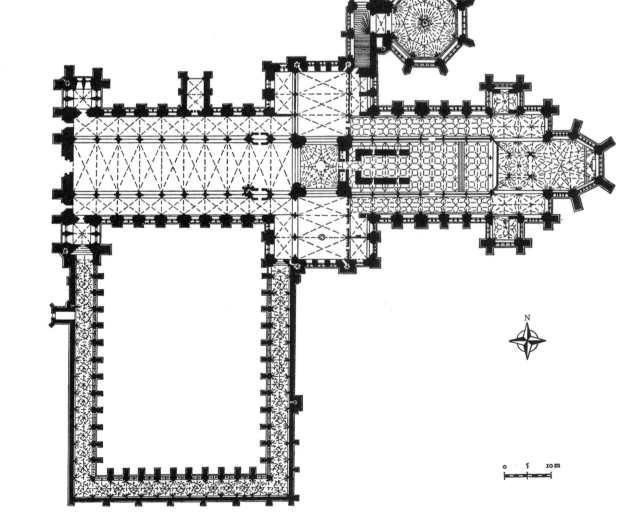

Total length	383 t.
Length of the choir	183 ft. 11 ⁴/₅ in.
Width of the nave and aisles . . .	68 ft. 1 ²/₅ in.
Width of the transept	134 ft. 11 ²/₃ in.
Width of the façade	147 ft. 0 ¹/₆ in.
Width of the nave alone	37 ft. 11 ⁹/₁₀ in.
Total width from arm of transept . .	68 ft. 12 in.
Height of inverted arches	47 ft. 0 ¹/₆ in.
Height of the façade up to the summit	
of the central gable	118 ft. 0 ¹/₈ in.
Height of the vault at wallside . . .	67 ft.

St. Peter's, Rome

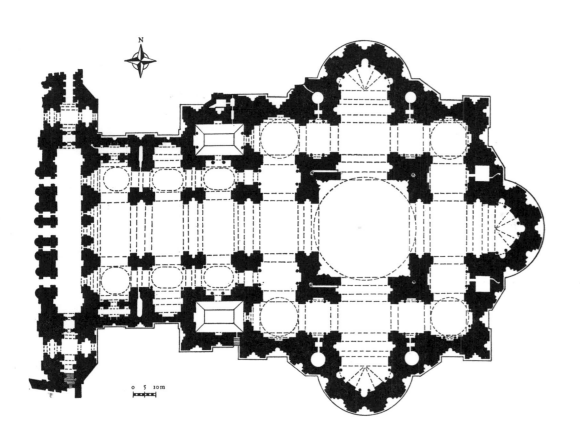

Total interiorl ength	613 ft.	6 $^1/_5$ in.
Length of the interior transept . . .	451 ft.	1 $^2/_5$ in.
Height of the cupola to summit of cross	434 ft.	8 $^1/_2$ in.
Diameter of the cupola	137 ft.	9 $^1/_2$ in.
Area	18 sq. yd. $^1/_5$	
Length of the façade	369 ft.	5 in.
Height of façade statues	18 ft.	8 $^2/_5$ in.
Interior height of the cupola	394 ft.	5 in.

Abbey of Our Lady, Zwiefalten

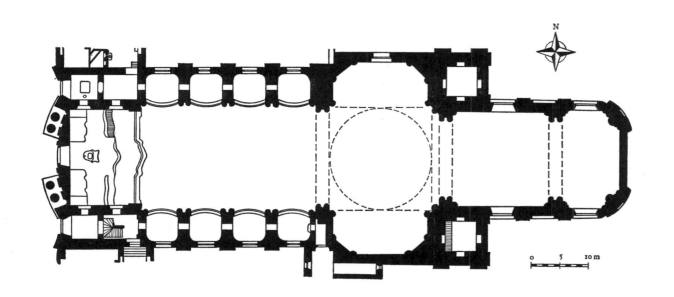

Length	298 ft.	6 $^2/_3$ in.
Width	95 ft.	1 $^3/_4$ in.
Height of the vaults	91 ft.	10 $^1/_3$ in.
Height of the façade	147 ft.	7 $^2/_3$ in.

Our Lady of All Grace, Assy

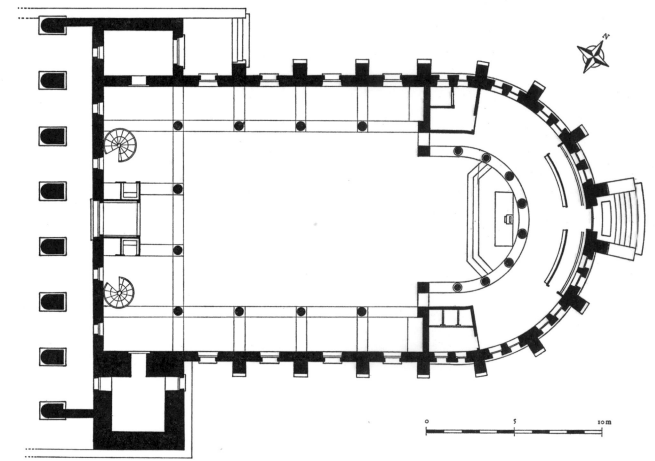

Total length	101 ft. 8 ¹/₂ in.
Length of the nave	59 ft. 0 ²/₃ in.
Width of the nave	48 ft. 2 ³/₄ in.
Width of the choir	23 ft. 5 ¹/₂ in.
Height of the façade gable	31 ft. 2 in.
Height of the campanile	103 ft. 0 ¹/₅ in.
Surface area of the Léger mosaic . .	137 sq. yd. ¹/₅
Surface area of the Lurçat tapisserie	
approx.	24 sq. yd. ⁴/₅

St. Michael's, Coventry

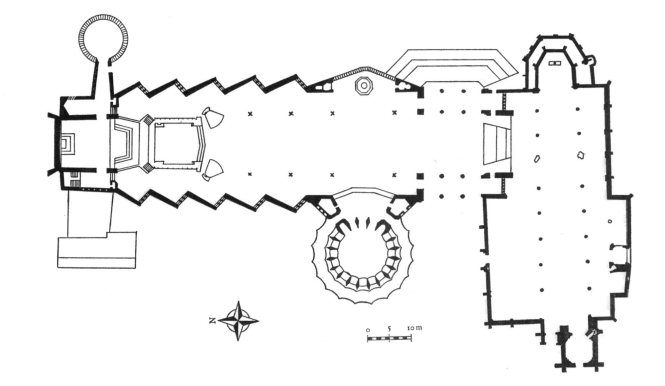

Total length	377 ft. 3 ¹/₂ in.
Length of the nave	249 ft. 1 ³/₅ in.
Width of the nave	88 ft. 7 in.
Width of the choir	46 ft. 6 ⁴/₅ in.
Height of the nave	73 ft. 9 ⁴/₅ in.
Tapestry by Sutherland :	
Height	77 ft. 11 ⁴/₅ in.
Width	37 ft. 12 in.

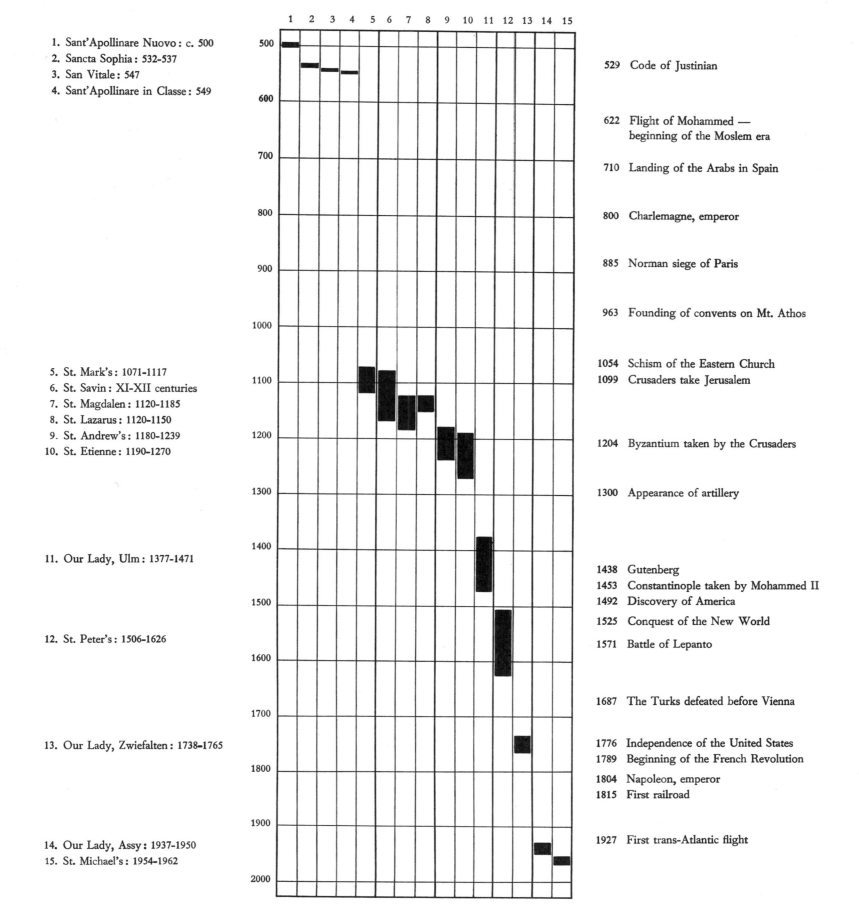

1. Sant'Apollinare Nuovo : c. 500
2. Sancta Sophia : 532-537
3. San Vitale : 547
4. Sant'Apollinare in Classe : 549

5. St. Mark's : 1071-1117
6. St. Savin : XI-XII centuries
7. St. Magdalen : 1120-1185
8. St. Lazarus : 1120-1150
9. St. Andrew's : 1180-1239
10. St. Etienne : 1190-1270

11. Our Lady, Ulm : 1377-1471

12. St. Peter's : 1506-1626

13. Our Lady, Zwiefalten : 1738-1765

14. Our Lady, Assy : 1937-1950
15. St. Michael's : 1954-1962

529   Code of Justinian

622   Flight of Mohammed —
        beginning of the Moslem era

710   Landing of the Arabs in Spain

800   Charlemagne, emperor

885   Norman siege of Paris

963   Founding of convents on Mt. Athos

1054 Schism of the Eastern Church
1099 Crusaders take Jerusalem

1204 Byzantium taken by the Crusaders

1300 Appearance of artillery

1438 Gutenberg
1453 Constantinople taken by Mohammed II
1492 Discovery of America

1525 Conquest of the New World

1571 Battle of Lepanto

1687 The Turks defeated before Vienna

1776 Independence of the United States
1789 Beginning of the French Revolution

1804 Napoleon, emperor
1815 First railroad

1927 First trans-Atlantic flight

LIST OF ILLUSTRATIONS

KEY:

Ar. = architecture	Mo. = mosaic	Sc. = sculpture	Sc. w. = wood sculpture
Orf. = gold work	Br. = bronze	Fr. = fresco	St. = stained glass